The Creative Curriculum® *for* Preschool

Teaching Guide
featuring the Trees Study

Kai-leé Berke, Carol Aghayan, Cate Heroman

TeachingStrategies® · Bethesda, MD

English editing: Lydia Paddock, Jayne Lytel
Design and layout: Jeff Cross, Amy Jackson, Abner Nieves
Spanish translation: Claudia Caicedo Núñez
Spanish editing: Judith F. Wohlberg, Alicia Fontán
Cover design: Laura Monger Design

Teaching Strategies, LLC
Bethesda, MD 20814

www.TeachingStrategies.com

978-1-60617-387-9

Library of Congress Cataloging-in-Publication Data

Berke, Kai-leé.
  The creative curriculum for preschool teaching guide featuring the trees study / Kai-leé Berke, Carol Aghayan, Cate Heroman.
     p. cm.
  ISBN 978-1-60617-387-9
  1. Education, Preschool--Activity programs. 2. Trees--Study and teaching (Preschool)--Activity programs. I. Aghayan, Carol. II. Heroman, Cate. III. Title.
  LB1140.35.C74B463 2010
  372.1102--dc22
                                    2010002154

Teaching Strategies, Creative Curriculum, LearningGames, GOLD, GOLDplus, Mighty Minutes, and Mega Minutos names and logos are registered trademarks of Teaching Strategies, LLC, Bethesda, MD. Brand-name products of other companies are suggested only for illustrative purposes and are not required for implementation of the curriculum.

8 9 10 11 12 13   23 22 21 20 19 18
    Printing   Year Printed

Printed and bound in China

Table of Contents

Getting Started

Why Investigate Trees?

Trees fascinate children and spark their curiosity and wonder. Close your eyes, and think of your childhood memories that involved trees. Did you ever climb a tree? Did you play chase and hide behind a tree? Did you lie down under a tree and wonder whether it touched the sky? Did you ever try to wrap your arms all the way around a tree? Did you wonder why there are holes in trees and what's inside them? Did you ever imagine what the world would be like without trees?

This study builds upon children's interest in trees to help them explore science and social studies. Rather than emphasize naming different trees, this study focuses on helping children develop an understanding of the characteristics of trees and their role in our natural and man-made worlds. During the study, children use skills in literacy, math, technology, and the arts to investigate and represent their knowledge about trees.

How do the children in your room show their interest in trees? What do they say about trees?

Web of Investigations

The Creative Curriculum® Teaching Guide featuring the Trees Study includes six investigations aimed at exploring trees. The investigations offer children an opportunity to learn more about the characteristics of trees and the role they play in our environment. Children will also learn about the creatures that inhabit trees and the foods trees produce.

Some of the investigations also include site visits and visits to the classroom from guest speakers. Each investigation helps children explore science and social studies and strengthens their skills in literacy, math, technology, and the arts. Expand this web by adding your own ideas, particularly about aspects of the topic that are unique to your community.

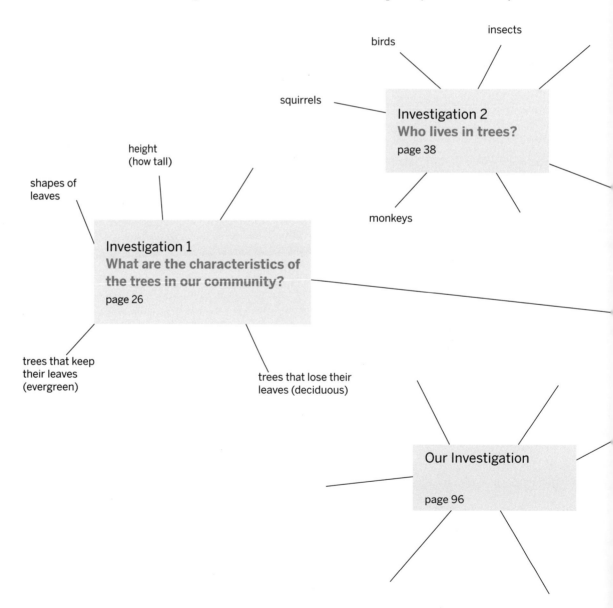

insects

birds

squirrels

Investigation 2
Who lives in trees?
page 38

monkeys

height
(how tall)

shapes of
leaves

Investigation 1
What are the characteristics of
the trees in our community?
page 26

trees that keep
their leaves
(evergreen)

trees that lose their
leaves (deciduous)

Our Investigation

page 96

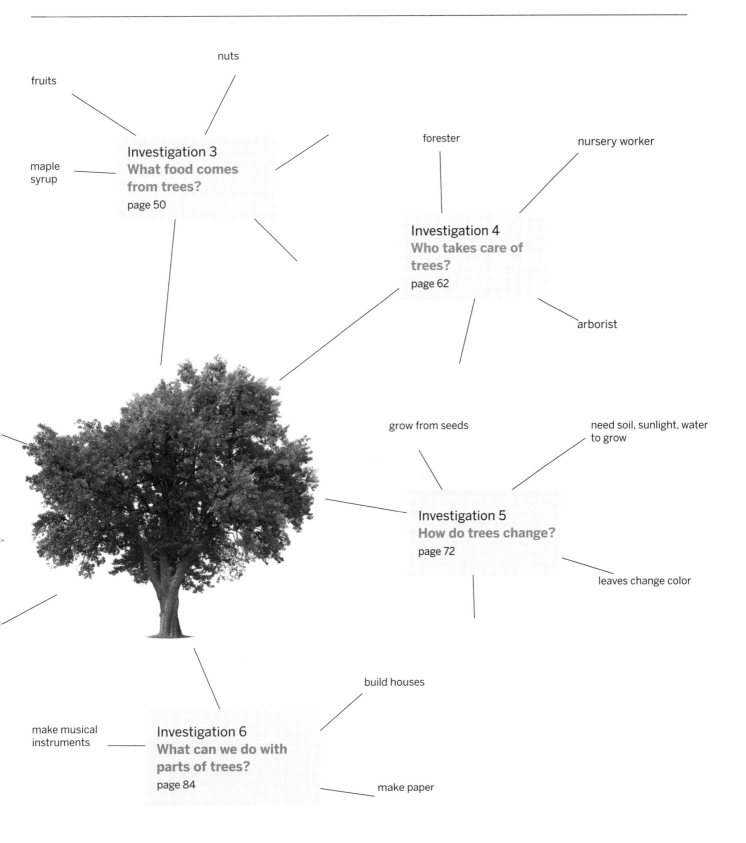

nuts

fruits

Investigation 3
What food comes from trees?
page 50

maple syrup

forester

nursery worker

Investigation 4
Who takes care of trees?
page 62

arborist

grow from seeds

need soil, sunlight, water to grow

Investigation 5
How do trees change?
page 72

leaves change color

build houses

make musical instruments

Investigation 6
What can we do with parts of trees?
page 84

make paper

A Letter to Families

Send families a letter introducing the study. Use the letter to communicate with families and as an opportunity to invite their participation in the study.

Dear Families,

Our class is beginning to study trees. We'll be observing and comparing trees to learn about what lives in them, what they're made from, and who cares for them. We hope that this study will help children explore and appreciate nature. As we study trees, we will use literacy, math, the arts, and technology to explore the topic in depth. We will learn important social studies and scientific concepts through firsthand investigations. Please visit the classroom during the study to see how we do this.

If you are able to take a "tree walk" with your child, we would appreciate your help in collecting tree parts to investigate. If you can, please take a bag to a tree area and collect things that have fallen, such as leaves, bark, acorns, twigs, flowers, fruit, or cones. See below for suggestions of other tree parts to bring in.

a variety of leaves	evergreen sprigs or	tree "cookies" (cross
small limbs, branches,	small boughs	sections of trees that
twigs	a live, potted tree	show the rings)
food from trees	flower clippings (may	bark
(fruit, nuts)	be kept in water)	
pinecones	seeds	

We need your help to enrich the children's learning. If you work with trees, please let us know. Perhaps you're a gardener, forester, tree trimmer, tree farmer, or nursery worker. Even if your job is unrelated to trees, you can be involved in our study. Extra hands always help!

What You Can Do at Home

You can help your child explore and appreciate nature by learning about trees. Invite your child to talk about trees. Share stories about your favorite childhood memories involving trees and games you might have played around them. Wonder aloud with your child to encourage his or her thinking about trees.

"I wonder why leaves fall from trees."

"I wonder what makes some trees grow so big."

At home, collect parts of trees, and encourage your child to sort them. Your child might also enjoy making a collage by arranging and gluing tree items on paper.

At the end of our study, we'll have a special event to show you what we learned. Thank you for playing an important role in our learning.

Carta a las familias

Envíe una carta a las familias para informarles sobre el estudio. Use la carta para comunicarse y como una oportunidad para invitarles a participar.

Apreciadas familias,

En nuestra clase estamos comenzando un estudio de los árboles. Vamos a observar y a comparar varios árboles en nuestra comunidad. Aprenderemos acerca de quiénes viven en los árboles, las distintas partes de los árboles y quién cuida de ellos. Esperamos que este estudio ayude a los niños a explorar y a apreciar la naturaleza. A medida que estudiemos los árboles, usaremos la lectoescritura, las matemáticas, las artes y la tecnología para explorar este tema en detalle. Además, por medio de investigaciones directas aprenderemos conceptos importantes de los estudios sociales y de la ciencia. Para que vean como lo hacemos, les invitamos a que visiten nuestro salón de clase durante el estudio.

De antemano agradecemos su ayuda, si pueden salir con sus niños en "búsqueda de árboles" para recolectar partes de árboles con el fin de investigarlas. Si pueden, por favor, lleven una bolsa a un área donde haya árboles y recolecten cosas que hayan caído de los árboles como hojas, corteza, bellotas, ramitas, flores, frutas o piñas. A continuación, ofrecemos sugerencias de varias partes de árboles para recolectar y traer a la escuela.

hojas de distintos árboles	semillas de pino (piñas)	flores cortadas (que
ramas de distintos tipos	ramas o ramitas de	puedan mantenerse
(pequeñas, delgadas,	árboles siempre verdes	en agua)
gruesas)	un árbol vivo, sembrado	cortes transversales
alimento producido por	en una maceta	(que muestren los
los árboles (frutas,	semillas	anillos de los árboles)
nueces)		corteza

Nosotros también necesitamos de su ayuda para enriquecer el aprendizaje de los niños de otras maneras. Si su trabajo está relacionado con los árboles, por favor infórmennos. Tal vez alguno de ustedes trabaje en jardinería, cuidado o mantenimiento de parques, arborización o tal vez sea especialista en árboles, arquitecto(a), agricultor(a) o trabaje en un invernadero. Incluso si no trabajan directamente con los árboles, por favor déjennos saber si desearían participar en nuestro estudio. ¡La ayuda adicional siempre es bienvenida!

Qué se puede hacer en el hogar

Ustedes pueden ayudar a sus niños a explorar y a apreciar la naturaleza aprendiendo de los árboles. Anímelos a hablar de los árboles y de su apariencia. Compartan los recuerdos de su infancia relacionados con los árboles y los juegos que tal vez jugaron cerca de ellos. Cuando estén en compañía de sus niños, pregúntense en voz alta para animarles a pensar en los árboles.

"Me pregunto por qué las hojas se caen de los árboles".

"Me pregunto por qué algunos árboles crecen tanto".

En casa, jueguen con los niños y exploren partes de árboles que hayan recolectado juntos. Ustedes podrán animar a sus niños a clasificar estos elementos. Sus niños también podrían disfrutar haciendo un collage, organizando y pegando partes de árboles en papel.

Al final de nuestro estudio, tendremos un evento especial para celebrar lo aprendido. De antemano, les agradecemos su participación y su importante rol en nuestro aprendizaje.

Beginning the Study

Introducing the Topic

To begin this study, you will explore the topic with the children to answer the following questions: What do we know about trees? What do we want to find out about trees?

Begin by collecting different parts of a tree. Ask the children, their families, and friends to help you build the collection. A sample letter to families is included in the beginning of this *Teaching Guide*. See the box below for suggestions on tree parts to gather.

Programs must be vigilant about poisonous tree parts and children's allergies. When exploring natural items, such as trees and the leaves, flowers, and food they produce, be mindful of toxins and whether they might trigger an allergic reaction. Take precautions to ensure everyone's safety.

Build on children's interest in trees as your tree collection arrives in the classroom. Think about how to store and display the collection. Make the items available for children to touch and explore. Children are going to be very interested in this growing collection, so make sure that they can examine the tree parts easily.

As tree parts begin to accumulate, start talking about them. Have children describe their colors, smells, and textures. Teach new vocabulary for naming and describing the items. Ask children to help you decide how to group the tree parts as you label and display them in the Discovery area.

> **What other open-ended questions or prompts can you use to stimulate discussion with children?**

a variety of leaves	pinecones	seeds
limbs, branches, twigs	evergreen sprigs or boughs	tree "cookies" (cross sections of trees that show the rings)
food from trees (fruit, nuts)	a live, potted tree	bark
	flower clippings (may be kept in water)	

Preparing For Wow! Experiences

The "At a Glance" pages list these suggested Wow! Experiences, which require some advance planning.

Exploring the Topic:	Day 2: A site visit to see trees
Investigation 1:	Day 2: A site visit to see trees
Investigation 2:	Day 2: A site visit to see trees
	Day 4: A visit from a family member to tell a story about something that lived in a tree
Investigation 3:	Day 3: A visit from someone who either grows food on trees or works with tree-grown food (If possible, arrange for the children to visit an orchard.)
Investigation 4:	Day 2: A visit from someone who takes care of trees
Investigation 6:	Day 2: A visit from a person who makes things out of wood
Celebrating Learning:	Day 2: Family members visit for the celebration. (For planting trees outdoors, contact your local forestry office or the Arbor Day Foundation to find out where to get free trees.)

Exploring the Topic

What do we know about trees? What do we want to find out?

Vocabulary—English: *bigger, smaller, same size, organize, inspiration*

	Day 1	Day 2	Day 3
Interest Areas	**Library:** books about trees	**Discovery:** collection of tree parts	**Discovery:** tree parts to sort and classify
Question of the Day	Did you see a tree on your way to school today?	Think about one tree very near your home or a tree you see on your way to school. Are you bigger or smaller than the tree?	Are you bigger or smaller than this tree? (Place a small potted tree near the question chart.)
Large Group	**Movement:** A Tree My Size **Discussion and Shared Writing:** The Sizes of Trees **Materials:** *Mighty Minutes* 49, "A Tree My Size"; several books about trees	**Song:** "The Green Grass Grows" **Discussion and Shared Writing:** What Will We See on Our Tree Hunt? **Materials:** *Mighty Minutes* 54, "The Green Grass Grows"; *Intentional Teaching Card* LL45, "Observational Drawing"; small clipboards; paper and pencils; digital camera	**Movement:** A Tree My Size **Discussion and Shared Writing:** What Do We Know About Trees? **Materials:** *Mighty Minutes* 49, "A Tree My Size"; collection of tree parts
Read-Aloud	*Our Tree Named Steve*	*Abiyoyo* *Book Discussion Card* 12 (first read-aloud)	*Chicka Chicka Boom Boom*
Small Group	**Option 1: Which Has More?** *Intentional Teaching Card* M19, "Which Has More?"; ice cube trays or egg cartons; resealable bags; collection of similarly sized objects, e.g., counters, coins, or colored chips **Option 2: Tall Towers** *Intentional Teaching Card* M59, "More or Fewer Towers"; interlocking cubes; more–fewer spinner; numeral–quantity cards or die	**Option 1: A Tree Poem** *Intentional Teaching Card* LL27, "Writing Poems"; audio recorder; *Gathering the Sun* **Option 2: Poetry and Photographs** *Intentional Teaching Card* LL27, "Writing Poems"; digital camera; audio recorder; computer; *Gathering the Sun*	**Option 1: Lining Up the Cubes** *Intentional Teaching Card* M31, "Lining It Up"; interlocking cubes **Option 2: Big and Small Tree Parts** *Intentional Teaching Card* M31, "Lining It Up"; collection of tree parts
Mighty Minutes®	*Mighty Minutes* 17, "Leaping Sounds"	*Mighty Minutes* 15, "Say It, Show It"; numeral cards	*Mighty Minutes* 60, "The Name Dance"

Day 4	Day 5	Make Time for…
Discovery: tree parts to sort and classify	**Art:** photos of a variety of trees	## Outdoor Experiences
Which of these comes from a tree? (Show three items, one of which comes from a tree.)	Which of these comes from a tree? (Show three items, one of which comes from a tree.)	**Physical Fun** • Use *Intentional Teaching Card* P15, "Dribble Kick." Follow the guidance on the card.

Outdoor Experiences

Physical Fun

- Use *Intentional Teaching Card* P15, "Dribble Kick." Follow the guidance on the card.

Family Partnerships

- Encourage families to take their children for a walk around their neighborhood to examine the trees they see. Give each family a small bag and ask them to help their children gather interesting parts that have fallen, such as leaves, twigs, acorns, nuts, and bark.

- Ask families to share memories with their children about when they were young and perhaps had memorable experiences with a tree, e.g., climbed a tree, enjoyed a picnic in the shade of a tree, or watched animals in trees. Ask them to send pictures if possible.

Wow! Experiences

- Day 2: A site visit to see trees

Visit trees in your play yard or community. Have the children count the trees and compare their sizes. Help them gather the leaves and sticks that they find, and take pictures comparing the children's heights to the trees' heights.

Day 4

Song: "The Green Grass Grows"

Discussion and Shared Writing: What Do We Know About Trees?

Materials: *Mighty Minutes* 54, "The Green Grass Grows"; photos from the tree hunt

Chicka Chicka Boom Boom

Option 1: Paint a Tree Picture

Intentional Teaching Card LL32, "Describing Art"; paints; ringed index cards with frequently used words and illustrations; *Colors! ¡Colores!*

Option 2: Tree Sculptures

Intentional Teaching Card LL32, "Describing Art"; modeling clay; *Colors! ¡Colores!*

Mighty Minutes 15, "Say It, Show It"; numeral cards

Day 5

Song: "The Green Grass Grows"

Discussion and Shared Writing: What Do We Want to Find Out About Trees?

Materials: *Mighty Minutes* 54, "The Green Grass Grows"

Abiyoyo
Book Discussion Card 12 (second read-aloud)

Option 1: Measuring Tree Parts

Intentional Teaching Card M12, "Measure & Compare"; nonstandard measuring tools; collection of sticks and leaves

Option 2: Measuring Outdoors

Intentional Teaching Card M12, "Measure & Compare"; nonstandard measuring tools; outdoor area with sticks and leaves; digital camera

Mighty Minutes 60, "The Name Dance"

13

What do we know about trees?
What do we want to find out?

Vocabulary

English: *bigger, smaller, same size*

Spanish: *más grande, más pequeño, del mismo tamaño*

Question of the Day: Did you see a tree on your way to school today?

Large Group

Opening Routine

- Sing a welcome song and talk about who's here.

> See *Beginning the Year Study* for more information and ideas about planning your opening routine. See *Intentional Teaching Card* SE02, "Look Who's Here!" for attendance chart ideas.

Movement: A Tree My Size

- Use *Mighty Minutes* 49, "A Tree My Size." Follow the guidance on the card.

- Write the *Mighty Minutes* 49 poem, "A Tree My Size," on chart paper.

- Display the chart. Point to the words as you read the poem.

Discussion and Shared Writing: The Sizes of Trees

- Review the question of the day located on the "At a Glance" chart. Invite children to describe the trees near their homes or those they saw on their way to school.

- Ask, "What does your tree look like? How big is your tree?"

- Record their responses.

- Draw a sketch of yourself (a simple stick figure). Then draw a tree that is *bigger* than your sketched figure, one that is *smaller*, and one that is the *same size*. Discuss the three sizes.

> During the first week of a new study, encourage the children's interest in the topic. Talk with the children to help them think about what they already know.

Before transitioning to interest areas, talk about the tree books in the Library area. Show a few pages from some of the books and point out interesting pictures and information.

Choice Time

As you interact with children in the interest areas, make time to do the following:

- Read books about trees with the children in the Library area. Pay attention to their interests.

- After reading, write brief notes about their ideas and questions.

> Spending time in the Library area encourages children's participation in this important interest area.

Read-Aloud

Read *Our Tree Named Steve*.

- **Before you read,** show the cover of the book, and read the title. Ask, "What do you think this book will be about?"

- **As you read,** allow time for the children to look at the illustrations on each page.

- **After you read,** help the children check their predictions and discuss their ideas.

Small Group

Option 1: Which Has More?

- Use *Intentional Teaching Card* M19, "Which Has More?" Follow the guidance on the card.

Option 2: Tall Towers

- Use *Intentional Teaching Card* M59, "More or Fewer Towers." Follow the guidance on the card.

Mighty Minutes®

- Use *Mighty Minutes* 17, "Leaping Sounds." Follow the guidance on the card.

Large-Group Roundup

- Recall the day's events.
- Tell children about tomorrow's site visit to see trees.

Day 2   Exploring the Topic

What do we know about trees?
What do we want to find out?

Vocabulary

English: See *Book Discussion Card* 12, *Abiyoyo, for words.*

Question of the Day: Think about one tree very near your home or a tree you see on your way to school. Are you bigger or smaller than the tree?

Large Group

Opening Routine

• Sing a welcome song and talk about who's here.

Song: "The Green Grass Grows"

• Use *Mighty Minutes* 54, "The Green Grass Grows." Follow the guidance on the card.

Discussion and Shared Writing: What Will We See on Our Tree Hunt?

• Review the question of the day. Invite children to describe the trees they chose and talk about their sizes.

• Explain, "Today we will be going on a tree hunt around our school."

• Ask, "What do you think we will see on our tree hunt?"

• Record the children's responses.

> For more information about helping children record their observations during a site visit, see *Intentional Teaching Card* LL45, "Observational Drawing." Remember to bring a camera with you to document this trip.

Before transitioning to interest areas, talk about the growing collection of tree parts in the Discovery area, and invite children to explore them during choice time.

Choice Time

As you interact with children in the interest areas, make time to do the following:

• Observe children as they explore the collection of tree parts.

• Pay attention to what interests them. Record their ideas and questions.

Read-Aloud

Read *Abiyoyo*.

- Use *Book Discussion Card* 12, *Abiyoyo*. Follow the guidance on the card for the first read-aloud.

> **Find a stick in the collection of tree parts to use as a "magic wand," similar to the one in the story. You can use your magic wand to dismiss children from large-group time, point to new materials as you introduce them, or announce cleanup time. Using an interesting prop can help get and keep children's attention, and it makes ordinary tasks fun!**

Small Group

Option 1: A Tree Poem

- Review *Intentional Teaching Card* LL27, "Writing Poems."

- Display the chart of the poem "A Tree My Size" from Day 1.

- Read the poem aloud. Share other poems that you have in the classroom, e.g., "Árboles/Trees" in *Gathering the Sun*.

- Follow the guidance on the card to help children create their own poetry.

Option 2: Poetry and Photographs

- Go on a nature walk with the children around the school grounds. Invite them to look for interesting trees.

- Have the children take photos of the trees they find.

- Return to the classroom, and view the photos together on the computer.

- Review *Intentional Teaching Card* LL27, "Writing Poems."

- Display the chart of the poem "A Tree My Size" from Day 1.

- Read the poem aloud. Share other poems that you have in the classroom, e.g., "Árboles/Trees" in *Gathering the Sun*.

- Help children create their own poetry inspired by their photos of trees.

Mighty Minutes®

- Use *Mighty Minutes* 15, "Say It, Show It." Follow the guidance on the card.

Large-Group Roundup

- Recall the day's events.

- Reflect on the site visit. Show any additional photos that you took today. Invite children to talk about what they observed during the tree hunt.

- Record their ideas. Tomorrow you will add them to the "What do we know about trees?" chart.

Day 3   Exploring the Topic

What do we know about trees?
What do we want to find out?

Vocabulary

English: *organize*

Spanish: *organizar*

Question of the Day: Are you bigger or smaller than this tree? (Place a small potted tree near the question chart.)

Large Group

Opening Routine

- Sing a welcome song and talk about who's here.

Movement: A Tree My Size

- Use *Mighty Minutes* 49, "A Tree My Size." Follow the guidance on the card.

> Encouraging children to make a movement for each word helps them separate a sentence into individual words.

Discussion and Shared Writing: What Do We Know About Trees?

- Have each child select an item from the collection of tree parts and pass it around for others to examine.

- Ask the following questions: "Do you know what that is? Where did it come from? How do you think it can be used?

Did you see anything like that on our tree hunt yesterday?"

- Create a chart called, "What do we know about trees?" Record some of the children's ideas and words on the chart. Add the children's ideas you recorded during yesterday's large-group roundup.

> If children bring in tree parts with berries or other materials that could be unsafe, e.g., sharp, splintered, allergenic, or potentially poisonous, put them in clear plastic jars with lids screwed on tightly and glued shut. This way the children can explore them and stay safe.

Before transitioning to interest areas, talk about the growing collection of tree parts in the Discovery area. Explain, "I need you to help me think of a way to *organize* the tree parts today during choice time."

Choice Time

As you interact with children in interest areas, make time to do the following:

- Ask, "What kinds of tree parts do we have?"

- Ask, "How can we *organize* these items?" If they need help, ask, "How are some of these tree parts the same? How are they different?"

- Invite children to sort the tree parts into categories.

- Review the question of the day.

- Invite children to sort some of the items by size.

Read-Aloud

Read *Chicka Chicka Boom Boom*.

- **Before you read,** show the cover of the book, and read the title aloud. Ask, "What is this story about?"

- **As you read,** emphasize the rhythm of the language.

- **After you read,** ask, "Do you think the other letters followed the letter *a* back up the coconut tree?"

Small Group

Option 1: Lining Up the Cubes

- Use *Intentional Teaching Card* M31, "Lining It Up."

- Follow the guidance on the card. Use interlocking cubes.

Option 2: Big and Small Tree Parts

- Use *Intentional Teaching Card* M31, "Lining It Up."

- Follow the guidance on the card. Use a collection of similar parts of trees, e.g., a collection of sticks or leaves.

Intentional Teaching Card **M31, "Lining It Up," is all about seriation, a way to arrange objects in a series or succession, e.g., by size.**

Mighty Minutes®

- Use *Mighty Minutes* 60, "The Name Dance." Follow the guidance on the card.

Large-Group Roundup

- Recall the day's events.

- Invite children who sorted tree parts during choice time to explain how they organized the collection.

What do we know about trees?
What do we want to find out?

Vocabulary

English: *organize*

Spanish: *organizar*

Question of the Day: Which of these comes from a tree?
(Show three items, one of which comes from a tree.)

Large Group

Opening Routine

- Sing a welcome song and talk about who's here.

Song: "The Green Grass Grows"

- Use *Mighty Minutes* 54, "The Green Grass Grows." Follow the guidance on the card.

- As you sing, sketch the tree parts on chart paper.

> "The Green Grass Grows" illustrates a growing pattern and is great for promoting memory skills. When children hear the same phrase repeatedly, they are more likely to join in. Drawing as you sing is helpful to all children, and the visual cues may help them participate.

Discussion and Shared Writing: What Do We Know About Trees?

- Review the chart, "What do we know about trees?"

- Remind children about their experiences organizing the collection of tree parts. Pass around photos from the tree hunt.

- Ask, "Is there anything else you'd like to add to our chart?"

- Record their ideas.

- Help the children state their ideas. For example, say, "Lani, you said your daddy planted a tree in a pot on your front stoop. Michael, you said you saw your neighbor plant a big tree in his front yard. Now we know that trees can be planted in pots and in the ground!"

- Review the question of the day.

English-Language Learners
When children begin to speak in sentences, do not correct their grammar. Be sure to model correct English.

Before transitioning to interest areas, talk about the collection of tree parts in the Discovery area and how children can continue to organize them.

Choice Time	As you interact with children in interest areas, make time to do the following: • Invite children to think of a way to *organize* and display the collection of tree parts in categories.	• Help children help make signs to label their categories.
Read-Aloud	Read *Chicka Chicka Boom Boom.* • **Before you read,** ask, "Who remembers what this story is about?" • **As you read,** sometimes pause and give children time to fill in rhyming words.	• **After you read,** open to the page listing the alphabet. Use it to transition children to the next activity. Point to the letters as you read them. For example, say, "This is a *B*. If your name starts with *B,* you may go wash your hands and sit down at the lunch table."

Small Group	**Option 1: Paint a Tree Picture** • Say, "Think about a tree that we saw on our tree hunt." • Invite children to talk about and then paint a picture of a tree. • Review *Intentional Teaching Card* LL32, "Describing Art." • Follow the guidance on the card. • Invite children to paint one of the trees they saw. • Share several tree-related poems from *Colors! ¡Colores!*	**Option 2: Tree Sculptures** • Say, "Think about a tree that we saw on our tree hunt." • Invite children to talk about and then sculpt a tree with modeling clay. • Review *Intentional Teaching Card* LL32, "Describing Art." • Follow the guidance on the card. • Invite children to sculpt one of the trees they saw. • Share several tree-related poems from *Colors! ¡Colores!* **Begin a display of the children's artwork on the study topic. They will have opportunities to add to the display as the study progresses.**

Mighty Minutes®	• Use *Mighty Minutes* 15, "Say It, Show It." Follow the guidance on the card.
Large-Group Roundup	• Recall the day's events. • Invite children to share their artwork with the group.

Day 5 Exploring the Topic

What do we know about trees?
What do we want to find out?

Vocabulary

English: *inspiration*; See *Book Discussion Card 12, Abiyoyo, for additional words.*

Spanish: *inspiración*

Question of the Day: Which of these comes from a tree?
(Show three items, one of which comes from a tree.)

Large Group

Opening Routine

- Sing a welcome song and talk about who's here.

Song: "The Green Grass Grows"

- Use *Mighty Minutes* 54, "The Green Grass Grows." Follow the guidance on the card.

- Invite children to create new verses to the song.

Discussion and Shared Writing: What Do We Want to Find Out About Trees?

- Review the question of the day. Add the children's responses to the chart, "What do we know about trees?"

- Post the chart near the large-group area for frequent reference.

- Say, "We already know a lot of things about trees. Now let's think about what we want to find out about trees."

- Model the questioning process for the children. For example, show them a few different kinds of pinecones and wonder aloud whether they all came from the same tree. Show them a leaf with a hole and wonder aloud how it got there.

- Record the children's questions.

- Help children formulate questions and extend their language. For example, if a child says, "I think we should grow trees at school," you might say, "You think we should grow trees at school. We'll need to know how to plant them and what to feed them. I'll write these questions on the chart:

    How do we plant trees?
    What do they need to grow?"

Before transitioning to interest areas, talk about the photos of trees in the Art area. Discuss how children can use them as inspiration—to get ideas—as they create their own art.

Choice Time

As you interact with children in the interest areas, make time to do the following:

- Talk to children about their artwork.

- Ask, "How did the tree photos inspire you? How did they give you *inspiration* for your artwork? How did they give you ideas?"

Read-Aloud

Read *Abiyoyo*.

- Use *Book Discussion Card* 12, *Abiyoyo*. Follow the guidance on the card for the second read-aloud.

Small Group

Option 1: Measuring Tree Parts

- Use *Intentional Teaching Card* M12, "Measure & Compare."

- Follow the guidance on the card. Use a collection of leaves and sticks.

Option 2: Measuring Outdoors

- Use *Intentional Teaching Card* M12, "Measure & Compare."

- Take the children and the materials outdoors.

- Follow the guidance on the card. Use tree parts that the children find outdoors.

- Photograph their found objects and measurements.

Mighty Minutes®

- Use *Mighty Minutes* 60, "The Name Dance." Try the variation on the back of the card.

Large-Group Roundup

- Recall the day's events.

- If the children participated in the outdoor experience during small-group time, share the photos that were taken while they were measuring. Invite children to talk about their discoveries.

Investigating the Topic

Introduction

You have already started lists of children's ideas and questions about trees. As you implement the study, you will design investigations that help the children expand their ideas, find answers to their questions, and learn important skills and concepts. This section has daily plans for investigating questions that children ask. Do not be limited by these suggestions. Use them as inspiration to design experiences tailored to your own group of children and the resources in your school and community. While it is important to respond to children's ideas and follow their lead as their thinking evolves, it is also important for you to organize the study and plan for possibilities.

Investigation 1

What are the characteristics of the trees in our community?

Vocabulary—English: *circumference, sturdy, senses, germs, poisonous, roots, trunk, crown, evergreen, deciduous, branch*

	Day 1	Day 2	Day 3
Interest Areas	**Art:** evergreen sprigs to be used as painting tools **Technology:** eBook version of *Trees Count*	**Discovery:** paper and crayons to make leaf rubbings; leaves; magnifying glasses	**Dramatic Play:** materials to construct a large tree
Question of the Day	What do you think we'll find under the trees on our site visit tomorrow?	How does this feel? (Display an interesting tree item.)	Which smells best to you? (Display two items from trees.)
Large Group	**Song:** "I'm a Sturdy Oak Tree" **Discussion and Shared Writing:** Preparing for the Site Visit **Materials:** *Mighty Minutes* 45, "I'm a Sturdy Oak Tree"; string; sphere, such as a ball, or cylinder, e.g., can or large wooden block	**Game:** Feely Box **Discussion and Shared Writing:** Using Our Senses to Explore Trees **Materials:** *Mighty Minutes* 48, "Feely Box"; feely box or bag; small paper bags; clipboards; paper and pencils; digital camera	**Game:** Riddle Dee Dee **Discussion and Shared Writing:** Examining Tree Parts **Materials:** *Mighty Minutes* 04, "Riddle Dee Dee"; collection of tree parts; *Trees, Trees, Trees*; paper and pencils; name cards
Read-Aloud	*Trees Count*	*Abiyoyo* *Book Discussion Card* 12 (third read-aloud)	*Our Tree Named Steve* *Intentional Teaching Card* SE05, "Character Feelings"
Small Group	**Option 1: Guessing Shapes** *Intentional Teaching Card* M20, "I'm Thinking of a Shape"; geometric solids; empty geometric-shaped containers **Option 2: Puzzles** *Intentional Teaching Card* M23, "Putting Puzzles Together"; puzzles or puzzle cards	**Option 1: Chicka Chicka ABC** *Intentional Teaching Card* LL34, "Alphabet Books"; *Chicka Chicka Boom Boom*; alphabet cards **Option 2: Big Tree ABC** *Intentional Teaching Card* LL34, "Alphabet Books"; *Chicka Chicka Boom Boom*; large tree made out of craft or butcher paper; letters made from construction paper	**Option 1: Alike and Different Leaves** *Intentional Teaching Card* M05, "Sorting & Classifying"; collection of leaves; objects that define boundaries for sorting **Option 2: Sorting Leaves** *Intentional Teaching Card* M05, "Sorting & Classifying"; collection of leaves; objects that define boundaries for sorting; digital camera
Mighty Minutes®	*Mighty Minutes* 55, "Mr. Forgetful"	*Mighty Minutes* 22, "Hot or Cold 3-D Shapes"; several three-dimensional shapes	*Mighty Minutes* 47, "Step Up" (Use the chart from today's large-group experience.)

Day 4	Day 5	Make Time for…
Toys and Games: several sets of matching leaf rubbings **Technology:** eBook version of *Trees, Trees, Trees*	**Toys and Games:** photos of trees to sort **Technology:** eBook version of *Trees Count*	## Outdoor Experiences **Plastic toy Hoop Corral** • Bring several plastic toy hoops outside and place them under trees. If plastic toy hoops aren't available, bring lengths of yarn or string to form a circle.
Have you ever seen a tree like this? (Display a photo of an *evergreen* tree.)	Have you ever seen a tree like this? (Display a photo of a *deciduous* tree.)	• Invite children to investigate *only* what they find in the space enclosed by the plastic toy hoop. • Give children magnifying glasses to look closely at what they find. Have them use clipboards, paper, and pencils to record their observations.
Song: "Ticky Ricky" **Discussion and Shared Writing:** Evergreen and Deciduous **Materials:** *Mighty Minutes* 12, "Ticky Ricky"; basket of assorted objects; *Trees, Trees, Trees*; photos from the tree hunt; tree parts; *Intentional Teaching Card* LL08, "Memory Games"	**Rhyme:** "Come Play With Me" **Discussion and Shared Writing:** Sharing Tree Photos **Materials:** *Mighty Minutes* 42, "Come Play With Me"; tree photos	**Physical Fun** • Use *Intentional Teaching Card* P17, "Balance on a Beam." Follow the guidance on the card. ## Family Partnerships • Invite a family member to visit the class during Investigation 2, "Who lives in trees?" Ask the family member to share an interesting story about an experience involving something that lived in a tree, e.g., watched a squirrel build a nest or saw baby birds hatch.
The Grouchy Ladybug Book Discussion Card 14 (first read-aloud)	*Trees Count*	• Ask families to bring or send in pictures of trees. • Invite families to access the eBooks, *Trees, Trees, Trees* and *Trees Count*.
Option 1: Creating Patterns *Intentional Teaching Card* M14, "Patterns"; objects for pattern making; pattern examples **Option 2: Tree Patterns** *Intentional Teaching Card* M14, "Patterns"; tree parts; pattern examples	**Option 1: Stick Letters** *Intentional Teaching Card* LL28, "Stick Letters"; collection of sticks; alphabet cards **Option 2: Stick Letter Books** *Intentional Teaching Card* LL28, "Stick Letters"; digital camera; collection of sticks; alphabet cards *Intentional Teaching Card* LL02, "Desktop Publishing"; computer; bookbinding materials; digital camera; printer; each child's word bank	## Wow! Experiences • Day 2: A site visit to see trees
Mighty Minutes 47, "Step Up" (Use the chart from yesterday's large-group experience.)	*Mighty Minutes* 22, "Hot or Cold 3-D Shapes"; assorted three-dimensional shapes	**Examine two to three different types of trees in or near the play yard. Focus on the parts of each tree as well as its smell, general shape, bark, color, and circumference. Tell the children what type (species) of tree they are examining. Collect twigs, leaves, and other items from a tree to add to the sand table. Take pictures and invite children to sketch their observations.**

What are the characteristics of the trees in our community?

Vocabulary

English: *circumference, sturdy*

Spanish: *circunferencia, resistente*

Question of the Day: What do you think we'll find under the trees on our site visit tomorrow?

Large Group

Opening Routine

- Sing a welcome song and talk about who's here.

Song: "I'm a Sturdy Oak Tree"

- Use *Mighty Minutes* 45, "I'm a Sturdy Oak Tree." Follow the guidance on the card.

- Explain the word *sturdy* before you sing the song.

English-Language Learners

When introducing a song, present the words first (without the melody). This approach makes it easier for children to hear each word. As often as possible, show pictures, or point to objects, that illustrate or explain unfamiliar words.

Discussion and Shared Writing: Preparing for the Site Visit

- Remind the children about tomorrow's site visit to closely investigate a few trees. Say, "We will look at the trees up close. We'll investigate them with magnifying glasses, record what we see, and collect items that we find on the ground underneath them."

- Read the question of the day, and record children's responses.

- Say, "We will also measure the *circumference* of each tree to find out how big around it is."

- Demonstrate how to measure *circumference* by using a piece of string and a sphere or cylinder.

Before transitioning to interest areas, talk about the evergreen sprigs in the Art area and how children can use them as painting tools.

Choice Time

As you interact with children in the interest areas, make time to do the following:

- Talk with them about their artwork.

- Ask questions that invite them to describe their work and explain the processes they used to create it. Say, for example, "I see several thin, wiggly lines in your painting. How did you make those?"

- Use rich vocabulary to describe what you see, e.g., "When you brushed the pine needles across your paper with paint, you made wispy marks."

English-Language Learners
When teaching a new word, such as *wispy*, put the word at or near the end of a sentence and emphasize it. Doing so is especially helpful for English-language learners. Use the new word as often as possible in this way. All learners of this age should acquire about 6 to 10 new words per day, and direct instruction is important.

Read-Aloud

Read *Trees Count*.

- **Before you read**, show the cover of the book, and read the title aloud. Ask, "What do you think this book is about?"

- **As you read**, point to the numeral as you read it.

- **After you read**, check the children's predictions, and discuss their ideas. Tell children that the book will be available on the computer in the Technology area.

Small Group

Option 1: Guessing Shapes

- Use *Intentional Teaching Card* M20, "I'm Thinking of a Shape."

- Follow the guidance on the card.

Option 2: Puzzles

- Review *Intentional Teaching Card* M23, "Putting Puzzles Together."

- Follow the guidance on the card.

Mighty Minutes®

- Use *Mighty Minutes* 55, "Mr. Forgetful." Follow the guidance on the card.

Large-Group Roundup

- Recall the day's events.

- Invite children who painted with tree parts during choice time to share their work.

What are the characteristics of the trees in our community?

Vocabulary

English: *senses, germs, poisonous*; See *Book Discussion Card* 12, *Abiyoyo, for additional words.*

Spanish: *sentidos, gérmenes, venenoso*

Question of the Day: How does this feel? (Display an interesting tree item.)

Large Group

Opening Routine

- Sing a welcome song and talk about who's here.

Game: Feely Box

- Use *Mighty Minutes* 48, "Feely Box."

- Review the question of the day.

- Follow the guidance on the card using tree parts.

Discussion and Shared Writing: Using Our Senses to Explore Trees

- Remind the children about the site visit.

- Ask, "How can we use our *senses* to explore trees today?" If the children need help, prompt them by asking, "How can we use our sense of smell?"

- Record their ideas.

- Talk about safety. Ask, "Why shouldn't we taste the tree parts?" Explain that parts of trees, bushes, and flowers are sometimes *poisonous* and might hurt people's bodies when they are eaten.

- Discuss things that they may touch and may not touch. For example, say, "Sometimes people throw trash on the ground. We might find it near our trees. We won't collect those items in our bags because they might be dangerous or have *germs* on them. We may collect leaves, sticks, and other items that have fallen from the tree."

- Talk about the importance of keeping the trees safe from harm, e.g., only pick up fallen tree parts, touch trees gently, and do not break off branches.

- Give each child a small paper bag, such as a lunch bag, that can be used for collecting tree parts. Distribute clipboards, paper, and pencils so the children can record what they see.

- Take photos to document this trip.

> Using paper bags to collect items on the site visit connects to an upcoming experience in which the children will explore papermaking. Demonstrate how to clip the top of the closed bag to the clipboard so it is easier to carry.

Before transitioning to interest areas, talk about the leaves and crayons in the Discovery area. Explain how to use them for leaf rubbings.

Choice Time

As you interact with children in the interest areas, make time to do the following:

- Observe children as they create leaf rubbings.

- Point out interesting features of the leaves and how they appear in the rubbings.

- Invite children to use magnifying glasses to look closely at the leaves and rubbings. Explain how to look closely and compare tiny details.

- Compare the veins that the children can see in the leaves with the veins they see in their hands and wrists.

Read-Aloud

Read *Abiyoyo*.

- Use *Book Discussion Card* 12, *Abiyoyo*. Follow the guidance on the card for the third read-aloud.

Small Group

Option 1: Chicka Chicka ABC

- Use *Intentional Teaching Card* LL34, "Alphabet Books."

- Follow the guidance on the card. Use *Chicka Chicka Boom Boom*.

Option 2: Big Tree ABC

- Create a large tree out of craft or butcher paper, and hang it on the wall within children's reach. Cut out the letters of the alphabet (uppercase and lowercase) from construction paper or write each letter on a piece of construction paper.

- Use *Intentional Teaching Card* LL34, "Alphabet Books."

- Follow the guidance on the card. Use *Chicka Chicka Boom Boom,* the large tree, and the letters you made.

- As you talk about each letter in the book, have a child attach that letter to the large tree.

English-Language Learners
As children are learning to produce letter sounds in English, accept and acknowledge their attempts without correcting errors. Continue to model correct pronunciation.

Mighty Minutes®

- Use *Mighty Minutes* 22, "Hot or Cold 3-D Shapes." Follow the guidance on the card.

Large-Group Roundup

- Recall the day's events.

- Discuss the site visit, and invite the children to share their discoveries.

What are the characteristics of the trees in our community?

Vocabulary

English: *senses, roots, trunk, crown*

Spanish: *sentidos, raíces, tronco, copa*

Question of the Day: Which smells best to you? (Display two items from trees.)

Large Group

Opening Routine

- Sing a welcome song and talk about who's here.

Game: Riddle Dee Dee

- Use *Mighty Minutes* 04, "Riddle Dee Dee."

- Follow the guidance on the card. Using children's name cards, try the syllable-jumping variation on the back.

Discussion and Shared Writing: Examining Tree Parts

- Review the question of the day.

- Examine a collection of tree items from yesterday's site visit. Invite children to use their *senses* to learn more about the items, e.g., smell the leaves, feel the bark, and look closely at the colors.

- Ask children to describe the items. Record what they say. (Save this chart for *Mighty Minutes* 47, "Step Up," later in the day.)

- If there is any evidence that something lives in the tree, point it out to children, and save or take a picture of it for the next investigation.

- Read the pages in *Trees, Trees, Trees* that describe the parts of the tree.

- Talk about the *roots*, *trunk*, and *crown* of the tree shown in the book. Explain what each part of the tree does, e.g., "The trunk moves water from the roots up to the leaves."

> **Give children paper and pencils or individual whiteboards and dry erase markers so they can sketch a tree and its parts as you read about them.**

Before transitioning to interest areas, talk about the materials in the Dramatic Play area that the children can use to create a large tree to hang on the wall.

Choice Time	As you interact with children in interest areas, make time to do the following: • Help children create a large tree on the wall in the Dramatic Play area. • Talk about the *roots*, *trunk*, and *crown* of the tree as they make each part.	
Read-Aloud	Read *Our Tree Named Steve*. • **Before you read**, ask, "What is this story about?" • **As you read**, talk about the feelings that the characters experience in the story. • **After you read**, ask, "How do you think the children felt when they came home?"	See *Intentional Teaching Card* **SE05**, **"Character Feelings," for tips on how to talk to children about the feelings of story characters.**
Small Group	**Option 1: Alike and Different Leaves** • Use *Intentional Teaching Card* M05, "Sorting & Classifying." • Follow the guidance on the card. Use a collection of leaves.	**Option 2: Sorting Leaves** • Review *Intentional Teaching Card* M05, "Sorting & Classifying." • Follow the guidance on the card. Use a collection of leaves. • Talk about the characteristics of the leaves as the children sort them, e.g., smooth, jagged, pointed, or curved edges; large or small; and their different colors and shapes. • Photograph the leaves and make a picture book.
Mighty Minutes®	• Use *Mighty Minutes* 47, "Step Up." Use the chart from today's large-group experience to circle a word. Follow the guidance on the card.	
Large-Group Roundup	• Recall the day's events.	• Invite children who created the large tree in the Dramatic Play area to share their work.

What are the characteristics of the trees in our community?

Vocabulary

English: *evergreen, deciduous*
Spanish: *árboles siempre verdes, de hojas caducas*
Question of the Day: Have you ever seen a tree like this?
(Display a photo of an *evergreen* tree.)

Large Group

Opening Routine

• Sing a welcome song and talk about who's here.

Song: "Ticky Ricky"

• Use *Mighty Minutes* 12, "Ticky Ricky."

• Follow the guidance on the card. Try the movement variation on the back.

Discussion and Shared Writing: Evergreen and Deciduous

• Read aloud pages 3–10 of *Trees, Trees, Trees*.

• Review the question of the day.

• Use the description in the book to talk about *evergreen* trees, which retain their leaves all year.

• Then use the description in the book to talk about *deciduous* trees, which lose their leaves.

• Create a chart with two sections. Record the characteristics of *deciduous* trees in one section and those of *evergreen* trees in another.

• Talk about the trees that the children saw on the site visit, and show them the photos from that visit.

• Help the children decide whether those trees stay green all year or lose their leaves.

• Examine tree parts that come from both *evergreen* and *deciduous* trees. Help the children sort the parts.

• Attach the photos and tree parts to the chart.

> The word *deciduous* may seem too complex to use with preschoolers. However, research shows that using unusual words in conversations is helpful for later literacy development.

Before transitioning to interest areas, talk about the leaf-rubbing matching game in the Toys and Games area and how children can use it. Tell children that *Trees, Trees, Trees* will be available on the computer in the Technology area.

> See *Intentional Teaching Card* **LL08, "Memory Games,"** for more information about supporting children's learning through matching games.

Choice Time

As you interact with children in the interest areas, make time to do the following:

- Observe them as they play the matching game with the leaf rubbings.

- Describe the leaves to help children pay attention to the details. For example, say, "You found a leaf with five points. Can you find another one with five points? These look similar. Let's count the points to see whether there are five."

English-Language Learners

Explaining what you or children are doing while you or they are doing it helps English-language learners engage in the activity and increase their vocabulary and comprehension. You might say, for example, "I count five points: one, two, three, four, five. There are five here, so this leaf matches that one."

Read-Aloud

Read *The Grouchy Ladybug*.

- Use *Book Discussion Card* 14, *The Grouchy Ladybug.* Follow the guidance on the card for the first read-aloud.

- Tell the children that the book will be available on the computer in the Technology area.

Small Group

Option 1: Creating Patterns

- Use *Intentional Teaching Card* M14, "Patterns." Follow the guidance on the card.

Option 2: Tree Patterns

- Use *Intentional Teaching Card* M14, "Patterns."

- Follow the guidance on the card. Use tree parts.

Mighty Minutes®

- Use *Mighty Minutes* 47, "Step Up." Use the chart from yesterday's large-group experience to circle a letter. Follow the guidance on the card.

Large-Group Roundup

- Recall the day's events.

- Invite the children to bring in photos or drawings of trees near their home.

To learn, children must connect new ideas and experiences with previous ideas and experiences. Help children recall their experiences each day to set the stage for new learning.

What are the characteristics of the trees in our community?

Vocabulary

English: *trunk, branch, crown, evergreen, deciduous*

Spanish: *tronco, rama, copa, árboles siempre verdes, de hojas caducas*

Question of the Day: Have you ever seen a tree like this?
(Display a photo of a *deciduous* tree.)

Large Group

Opening Routine

- Sing a welcome song and talk about who's here.

Rhyme: "Come Play With Me"

- Use *Mighty Minutes* 42, "Come Play With Me." Follow the guidance on the card.

Discussion and Shared Writing: Sharing Tree Photos

- Review the question of the day.
- Invite children to share their photos of trees near their homes.
- Ask the children to describe their trees.
- Record their descriptions.

- Point out how the individual trees' *trunks, branches,* and *crowns* look different.
- Ask, "Does this look like a tree that stays green all year? Is it an *evergreen* tree? Does it look like a tree that loses its leaves? Is it a *deciduous* tree?"

> Talk informally about letters and their sounds as you write them, e.g., "Tree starts with the /tr/ sounds. We use the letters *t* and *r* to write these sounds. Triangle starts with the /tr/ sounds, too. Watch how I write *t, r.*"

Before transitioning to interest areas, talk about the tree photos in the Toys and Games area and how children can sort them.

Choice Time

As you interact with children in the interest areas, make time to do the following:

- Observe children as they examine and sort the photos in the Toys and Games area.
- Ask questions to encourage them to explain their groupings.

English-Language Learners

Give all children time to express themselves.

Read-Aloud

Read *Trees Count*.

- **Before you read**, tell children to look closely at the trees in the illustrations for any that they have seen in the community.

- **As you read**, invite the children to discuss the characteristics of the trees.

- **After you read**, compare children's photos, or drawings, of trees to the pictures of the trees in the book. Talk about similarities and differences, e.g., "Marcus's tree has flowers like this magnolia tree."

Small Group

Option 1: Stick Letters

- Review *Intentional Teaching Card* LL28, "Stick Letters." Follow the guidance on the card.

Option 2: Stick Letter Books

- Review *Intentional Teaching Card* LL28, "Stick Letters." Follow the guidance on the card.

- Take photos of the children's letter creations. Use the photos to create an alphabet book.

See *Intentional Teaching Card* **LL02, "Desktop Publishing," for more ideas about using photos of children's stick letters in a book.**

Mighty Minutes®

- Use *Mighty Minutes* 22, "Hot or Cold 3-D Shapes." Follow the guidance on the card.

Large-Group Roundup

- Recall the day's events.

- If you took photos of children's stick letters, share them with the group. For example, say, "Jamal made a special letter. It is the first letter in his name. Can you tell me what letter he made?"

Investigation 2

Who lives in trees?

Vocabulary—English: *clue, senses, harmful, helpful, sturdy*

	Day 1	Day 2	Day 3
Interest Areas	**Art:** materials to make bark rubbings; magnifying glass **Technology:** eBook version of *Who Lives in Trees?*	**Discovery:** tree parts, magnifying glasses **Technology:** eBook version of *Who Lives in Trees?*	**Discovery:** tree parts, magnifying glasses
Question of the Day	Which animal lives in a tree: an alligator or a squirrel?	Who might have made this home in a tree? (Display a bird's nest or photo of one.)	Could this insect hurt a tree? (Display the picture of the pine beetle from *Who Lives in Trees?*)
Large Group	**Song:** "Strolling Through the Park" **Discussion and Shared Writing:** Who Might Live in Our Trees? **Materials:** *Mighty Minutes* 46, "Strolling Through the Park"; *Who Lives in Trees?* *Intentional Teaching Card* SE11, "Great Groups"	**Game:** Riddles **Discussion and Shared Writing:** Preparing for the Site Visit **Materials:** *Mighty Minutes* 61, "Riddle, Riddle, What Is That?"; evidence that a creature lives in a tree	**Game:** Let's Pretend **Discussion and Shared Writing:** Harmful and Helpful **Materials:** *Mighty Minutes* 39, "Let's Pretend"; *Who Lives in Trees?*; *The Grouchy Ladybug*; evidence that a creature lives in a tree
Read-Aloud	*The Grouchy Ladybug* *Book Discussion Card* 14 (second read-aloud)	*Who Lives in Trees?*	*The Grouchy Ladybug* *Book Discussion Card* 14 (third read-aloud)
Small Group	**Option 1: How Many Are in the Tree?** *Intentional Teaching Card* M22, "Story Problems"; collection of creatures that live in trees **Option 2: Big Story Problems** *Intentional Teaching Card* M22, "Story Problems"; collection of tree-living creatures; masking tape or butcher paper	**Option 1: Show Me Five** *Intentional Teaching Card* M16, "Show Me Five"; collection of small objects **Option 2: Nursery Rhyme Count** *Intentional Teaching Card* M13, "Nursery Rhyme Count"; cotton balls; green construction paper; numeral cards	**Option 1: Rhyming Riddles** *Intentional Teaching Card* LL11, "Rhyming Riddles"; props that rhyme with chosen words **Option 2: Rhyming Tubs** *Intentional Teaching Card* LL44, "Rhyming Tubs"; plastic tub; bag or small box; pairs of small objects with names that rhyme
Mighty Minutes®	*Mighty Minutes* 25, "Freeze"; dance music; letter cards	*Mighty Minutes* 60, "The Name Dance"	*Mighty Minutes* 44, "Two Plump Armadillos"

Day 4	Day 5	Make Time for…
Dramatic Play: realistic animal puppets	**Dramatic Play:** realistic animal puppets; materials for building tree homes	## Outdoor Experiences **Who Lives in Trees?** • Bring binoculars and magnifying glasses outdoors for the children to use. Invite them to look for insects and other animals in the trees. **Physical Fun** • Use *Intentional Teaching Card* P16, "Body Part Balance." Follow the guidance on the card.
Does this animal live in a tree? (Show an image of an animal that doesn't live in trees.)	What creature lives in this tree home? (Display a photo of a hive.)	
Song: "I'm a Sturdy Oak Tree" **Discussion and Shared Writing:** Tree Storytelling **Materials:** *Mighty Minutes* 45, "I'm a Sturdy Oak Tree"; *Who Lives in Trees?*	**Song:** "Strolling Through the Park" **Discussion and Shared Writing:** Homes in Trees **Materials:** *Mighty Minutes* 46, "Strolling Through the Park"; *Who Lives in Trees?*	## Family Partnerships • Invite children to ask their families about experiences they have had with insects or other animals in trees. • Invite a family member or another community member who grows food on trees, e.g., a farmer or someone with a fruit tree at home, to visit the class during Investigation 3, "What food comes from trees?" • If you can't find anyone who grows or harvests food on trees, invite someone who works with tree-grown food, e.g., grocery store produce manager, cook, or cafeteria server.
When the Monkeys Came Back	*Henny Penny* *Book Discussion Card* 15 (first read-aloud)	
Option 1: Creature Paintings *Intentional Teaching Card* LL32, "Describing Art"; paint; index cards with frequently used words and illustrations **Option 2: Animal Sculptures** *Intentional Teaching Card* LL32, "Describing Art"; modeling clay; index cards with frequently used words and illustrations	**Option 1: Spy Outside** *Intentional Teaching Card* LL01, "Shared Writing"; book with tree photos **Option 2: Investigating Animal Homes** *Intentional Teaching Card* LL63, "Investigating & Recording"; small clipboards; paper; pencils	## Wow! Experiences • Day 2: A site visit to see trees --- **Revisit the trees in the neighborhood or play yard that the children have examined during previous investigations. Look for evidence of animal or insect inhabitants.** --- • Day 4: A visit from a family member to tell a story about something that lived in a tree
Mighty Minutes 89, "We Like Clapping"	*Mighty Minutes* 62, "Where Can He Be?"	

Investigation 2

Who lives in trees?

Vocabulary

English: *See Book Discussion Card 14, The Grouchy Ladybug (La mariquita malhumorada),* for words.

Question of the Day: Which animal lives in a tree: an alligator or a squirrel?

Large Group

Opening Routine

- Sing a welcome song and talk about who's here.

Song: "Strolling Through the Park"

- Use *Mighty Minutes* 46, "Strolling Through the Park." Follow the guidance on the card.

- Say the rhyme a second time. Pause to give children time to fill in rhyming words.

> **For more information on conducting large-group time see,** *Intentional Teaching Card* **SE11, "Great Groups."**

Discussion and Shared Writing: Who Might Live in Our Trees?

- Review the question of the day.

- Read *Who Lives in Trees?*

- On chart paper, list the creatures in the book that live in trees.

- Wonder aloud, "What might live in our trees? How can we find out?"

- Record the children's responses. Save the chart for tomorrow's read-aloud activity.

Before transitioning to interest areas, talk about the bark in the Discovery area and how to make bark rubbings. Tell children that the book will be available on the computer in the Technology area.

Choice Time

As you interact with children in the interest areas, make time to do the following:

- Observe children as they make bark rubbings in the Discovery area.

- Invite children to use a magnifying glass to look closely at the bark. Help them compare it with their rubbings.

Read-Aloud

Read *The Grouchy Ladybug*.

- Use *Book Discussion Card* 14, *The Grouchy Ladybug*. Follow the guidance on the card for the second read-aloud.

Small Group

Option 1: How Many Are in the Tree?

- Use *Intentional Teaching Card* M22, "Story Problems."

- Follow the guidance on the card. Create stories about creatures that live in trees.

Option 2: Big Story Problems

- Use masking tape or butcher paper to create a large tree on the floor or ground.

- Use *Intentional Teaching Card* M22, "Story Problems."

- Follow the guidance on the card. Create stories about creatures that live in trees.

- Invite the children to pretend to be the creatures in the story. For example, you might say, "Five squirrels were hiding in the tree." Have five children go and stand on the tree. Then say, "Two squirrels jumped out to get some nuts." Have two children jump out of the tree. Ask, "How many are still in the tree?"

> Acting out story problems like this helps build the foundation for children's understanding of addition and subtraction.

Mighty Minutes®

- Use *Mighty Minutes* 25, "Freeze." Try the letter variation on the back of the card.

Large-Group Roundup

- Recall the day's events.

- Invite children who made bark rubbings in the Discovery area to share their work.

Who lives in trees?

Vocabulary

English: *clue, senses*

Spanish: *pista, sentidos*

Question of the Day: Who might have made this home in a tree? (Display a bird's nest or photo of one.)

Large Group

Opening Routine

- Sing a welcome song and talk about who's here.

Game: Riddles

- Use *Mighty Minutes* 61, "Riddle, Riddle, What Is That?" Follow the guidance on the card.

Discussion and Shared Writing: Preparing for the Site Visit

- Explain, "We know from the stories we've read and some of your ideas that some creatures live in trees. Let's look at some tree parts for *clues* that will tell us if something lives in our trees."

- Review the question of the day.

- Display an item from the previous site visit that shows evidence that animals live in or near a tree, e.g., a partially eaten leaf, a clump of twigs that looks as though it came from a nest, or a feather. If nothing like that turned up on the site visit, bring something from a tree located elsewhere.

- Describe the item and the *clue* it provides. For example, you might say, "This leaf has some holes in it. That is a *clue* that something might be living in our tree—something that eats leaves."

- Remind children about the site visit.

- Ask, "Which of our *senses* will we use today to collect information about what lives in our trees?"

- Ask, "What *clues* will we look for to tell us that something lives in the trees?"

- Record the children's responses.

Before transitioning to interest areas, talk about the collection of tree parts in the Discovery area. Discuss how the children can examine them for *clues* that something is, or was, living in the trees.

> **For more information on introducing new vocabulary words to children, see *Intentional Teaching Card*, LL43 "Introducing New Vocabulary."**

Choice Time	As you interact with children in the interest areas, make time to do the following: • Observe their investigations of the tree parts. • Record their discoveries and ideas.

Read-Aloud

Read *Who Lives in Trees?*

• **Before you read**, show the cover and tell children the name of the book. Ask, "What do you think this book is about?"

• **As you read**, pause and give children time to recall the animal names.

• **After you read**, refer to the list you made yesterday during large-group time. Review the animals that live in trees. Ask, "What animals do not live in trees?" Add a column to the chart and record the children's responses. Tell the children that the book will be available on the computer in the Technology area.

Small Group

Option 1: Show Me Five

• Use *Intentional Teaching Card* M16, "Show Me Five." Follow the guidance on the card.

Option 2: Nursery Rhyme Count

• Use *Intentional Teaching Card* M13, "Nursery Rhyme Count." Follow the guidance on the card.

Mighty Minutes®

• Use *Mighty Minutes* 60, "The Name Dance." Follow the guidance on the card.

Large-Group Roundup

• Recall the day's events.

• Invite children to share their observations from today's site visit.

Day 3 Investigation 2

Who lives in trees?

Vocabulary

English: *harmful, helpful*

Spanish: *perjudicial, beneficioso*

Question of the Day: Could this insect hurt a tree? (Display the picture of the pine beetle from *Who Lives in Trees?*)

Large Group

Opening Routine

- Sing a welcome song and talk about who's here.

Game: Let's Pretend

- Use *Mighty Minutes* 39, "Let's Pretend."

- Follow the guidance on the card.

- Invite children to pretend to be birds, e.g., fly through the air, land on trees, or build nests.

Discussion and Shared Writing: Harmful and Helpful

- Show children the first and last few pages of *The Grouchy Ladybug*.

- Remind them about the aphids and that the leaf was grateful when the ladybugs ate all of the aphids.

- Explain, "Aphids are tiny bugs that can hurt the leaves on trees and other plants. Aphids are *harmful* to trees. The ladybug helped the tree by eating the aphids. Ladybugs are *helpful* to trees."

- Review the question of the day.

- Show the picture of the pine beetle in *Who Lives in Trees?* Explain, "A pine beetle is a small insect about the size of a grain of rice. Pine beetles are *harmful* to trees because they make holes through the bark and lay eggs. When the eggs hatch, the baby beetles eat the wood underneath the bark. The tree will die if the beetles eat too much wood."

- Pass around some of the items from the tree collection that the children previously identified as being clues that something lives in the tree. Have them look carefully at the items.

- Ask, "Do you think that whatever is living in the tree is *harmful* or *helpful*? Why?"

- Record their responses.

Before transitioning to interest areas, talk about the collection of tree parts in the Discovery area. Discuss how children can examine them for clues that something is or was living in the trees.

Choice Time	As you interact with children in the interest areas, make time to do the following:
	• Observe their investigations of tree parts.
	• Record their discoveries and ideas.

Read-Aloud	Read *The Grouchy Ladybug*.	**English-Language Learners**
	• Use *Book Discussion Card* 14, *The Grouchy Ladybug.* Follow the guidance on the card for the third read-aloud.	Rereading books several times helps all learners gain an understanding of unfamiliar words and phrases.
	• Tell the children that the book will be available on the computer in the Technology area.	

Small Group	**Option 1: Rhyming Riddles**	**Option 2: Rhyming Tubs**
	• Use *Intentional Teaching Card* LL11, "Rhyming Riddles."	• Use *Intentional Teaching Card* LL44, "Rhyming Tubs."
	• Follow the guidance on the card. Use trees, tree parts, and creatures who live in trees.	• Follow the guidance on the card. Use the word *tree*.

Mighty Minutes®	• Use *Mighty Minutes* 44, "Two Plump Armadillos." Follow the guidance on the card.

Large-Group Roundup	• Recall the day's events.
	• Remind children that a family or community member will be visiting the class tomorrow to tell a story about something that lived in a tree.

Who lives in trees?

Vocabulary

English: *sturdy*

Spanish: *resistente*

Question of the Day: Does this animal live in a tree? (Show an image of an animal that doesn't live in trees.)

Large Group

Opening Routine

- Sing a welcome song and talk about who's here.

Song: "I'm a Sturdy Oak Tree"

- Use *Mighty Minutes* 45, "I'm a Sturdy Oak Tree."

- Ask, "Does anybody remember what *sturdy* means?" Remind the children of the definition.

- Follow the guidance on the card. Try including animals with the examples on the back of the card.

Discussion and Shared Writing: Tree Storytelling

- Introduce the visiting family or community member, or invite the related child to introduce the visitor.

- Invite the visitor to share his or her tree story with the children.

- Encourage the children to ask questions and listen to the answers.

Before transitioning to interest areas, talk about the animal puppets in the Dramatic Play area. Review the question of the day. Ask, "Which of these puppets look like creatures that live in trees?"

Choice Time

As you interact with children in the interest areas, make time to do the following:

- Invite children to use the large tree in the Dramatic Play area as they play with the animal puppets.

- Listen to find out what children already know about the homes of those creatures. Record their ideas and save them for tomorrow's large-group time.

Read-Aloud

Read *When the Monkeys Came Back.*

- **Before you read**, show the cover and tell children the name of the book. Say, "If the monkeys came back, I wonder if that means they first went away." Ask, "Where do you think monkeys live? What do you think made them leave?"

- **As you read**, help children keep track of the story events over time. Stop periodically and briefly summarize what has happened so far.

- **After you read**, recall children's predictions and discuss whether they were correct. Ask, "What did Doña Marta do to help the monkeys come back? What would you have done?"

Small Group

Option 1: Creature Paintings

- Review *Intentional Teaching Card* LL32, "Describing Art."

- Follow the guidance on the card.

- Invite children to create a painting of an insect or another animal that lives in trees.

Option 2: Animal Sculptures

- Review *Intentional Teaching Card* LL32, "Describing Art."

- Follow the guidance on the card.

- Invite children to use modeling clay to create a sculpture of an insect or another animal that lives in trees.

Add children's paintings or sculptures to the display of children's representations that started during the first week of this study.

Mighty Minutes®

- Use *Mighty Minutes* 89, "We Like Clapping." Use children's ideas to vary the movements.

Large-Group Roundup

- Recall the day's events.
- Write a group thank-you note to the family or community member who shared a tree story.

Who lives in trees?

Vocabulary

English: *See Book Discussion Card 15, Henny Penny, (Pollita Pequeñita), for words.*

Question of the Day: What creature lives in this tree home? (Display a photo of a hive.)

Large Group

Opening Routine

- Sing a welcome song and talk about who's here.

Song: "Strolling Through the Park"

- Use *Mighty Minutes* 46, "Strolling Through the Park."

- Follow the guidance on the card. Pause to allow children to fill in rhyming words.

Discussion and Shared Writing: Homes in Trees

- Explain, "We've discovered a lot about the kinds of insects and other animals that live in trees."

- Review the question of the day.

- Ask, "What kinds of homes do those insects and other animals make in trees?" (Possible answers include nests, dens, hives, webs.)

- Record the children's responses.

- Talk about the kinds of animals that make homes in trees.

- If needed, prompt the children's thinking by looking at pictures and finding clues in *Who Lives in Trees?*

Before transitioning to interest areas, talk about the puppets and materials for building tree homes in the Dramatic Play area. Discuss how the children can use them.

> During choice time, take advantage of video footage on the Internet to show children nests and the other homes of creatures that live in trees.

Choice Time

As you interact with children in the interest areas, make time to do the following:

- Observe their play with puppets. Listen and look for how children demonstrate their learning about the study topic, e.g., a child plays with a squirrel puppet and pretends to gather sticks to make a nest.

- Ask, "What materials in our room could we use to make a web for your spider? Will you help me find some?"

- Help children attach their animal homes to the tree.

English-Language Learners
When English-language learners interact with their peers during choice-time activities and listen to you and other children speak English, they continue to develop important oral language skills.

Read-Aloud

Read *Henny Penny.*

- Use *Book Discussion Card* 15, *Henny Penny*. Follow the guidance on the card for the first read-aloud.

- Tell the children that the book will be available on the computer in the Technology area.

Small Group

Option 1: I Spy Outside

- Use *Intentional Teaching Card* LL01, "Shared Writing."

- Play a game of "I Spy..." outside. Use things you see on and around trees, e.g., "I spy something small and round on the tree trunk." If you can't go outside, use a book with photos of trees.

- Invite the children to take turns spying and giving clues.

- Record their clues and observations on the chart.

- When you are finished with the game, review the chart with the children.

Option 2: Investigating Animal Homes

- Use *Intentional Teaching Card* LL63, "Investigating & Recording."

- Follow the guidance on the card.

- Invite the children to look for animal homes in the trees they find outdoors.

Mighty Minutes®

- Use *Mighty Minutes* 62, "Where Can He Be?" Use an animal that lives in a tree.

Large-Group Roundup

- Recall the day's events.

- Invite children to share what they discovered about trees during small-group time today.

Investigation 3

What food comes from trees?

Vocabulary—English: *weigh, scale, heavier, lighter, acorn, stretch, reach, lean, twist, flip, slide, roll*

	Day 1	Day 2	Day 3
Interest Areas	**Library:** books about tree-grown foods and the animals that eat them	**Discovery:** scale, tree parts **Technology:** eBook version of *Who Lives in Trees?*	**Art:** materials to make a collage **Technology:** eBook version of *Henny Penny*
Question of the Day	Did this grow on a tree? (Display a fruit or nut from a tree.)	Did this grow on a tree? (Display a different fruit or nut from a tree.)	Did this grow on a tree? (Display an apple.)
Large Group	**Song:** "Strolling Through the Park" **Discussion and Shared Writing:** Why Do Animals Live in Trees? **Materials:** *Mighty Minutes* 07, "Hippity, Hoppity, How Many?"	**Rhyme:** "High in the Tree" **Discussion and Shared Writing:** Food Grown on Trees **Materials:** *Mighty Minutes* 51, "High in the Tree"; sentence strips; pictures of trees and their fruits and nuts; list of tree-grown foods the children generated yesterday	**Song:** "Strolling Through the Park" **Discussion and Shared Writing:** Visitor Who Grows Food on Trees **Materials:** *Mighty Minutes* 46, "Strolling Through the Park"; samples of food grown on trees; *Growing Trees*
Read-Aloud	*Henny Penny* *Book Discussion Card* 15 (second read-aloud)	*Who Lives in Trees?* list of tree-grown foods	*Henny Penny* *Book Discussion Card* 15 (third read-aloud)
Small Group	**Option 1: I Went Shopping** *Intentional Teaching Card* LL31, "I Went Shopping"; 5–6 pieces of print found in a grocery store; grocery bag **Option 2: What's for Snack?** *Intentional Teaching Card* LL25, "What's for Snack?"; food product labels; large paper or tagboard; recipe cards or chart	**Option 1: Nonsense Names** *Intentional Teaching Card* LL10, "Rhyming Chart"; *Henny Penny;* props that illustrate the study **Option 2: Rhyming Riddles** *Intentional Teaching Card* LL11, "Rhyming Riddles"; props that rhyme with chosen words	**Option 1: Applesauce** *Intentional Teaching Card* M28, "Applesauce" (See card for equipment, recipe, and ingredients.) **Option 2: Apple Bread** *Intentional Teaching Card* M29, "Apple Bread" (See card for equipment, recipe, and ingredients.)
Mighty Minutes®	*Mighty Minutes* 44, "Two Plump Armadillos"	*Mighty Minutes* 10, "Words in Motion"	*Mighty Minutes* 04, "Riddle Dee Dee"; numeral cards

Spanish: *pesa, báscula, más pesado, más liviano, bellota, estirarse, alcanzar, apoyarse, torcer, voltear, deslizar, rodar*

Day 4	Day 5	Make Time for...
Art: illustrations of new *Henny Penny* characters **Technology:** eBook version of *Trees Count*	**Dramatic Play:** props to act out *Henny Penny* **Technology:** eBook version of *Henny Penny*	## Outdoor Experiences ### Leaf Silhouettes
Is *Henny Penny* a real story or pretend?	Which food tastes best to you? (Offer samples of two tree-grown foods.)	
Rhyme: "High in the Tree" **Discussion and Shared Writing:** *Henny Penny* **Materials:** *Mighty Minutes* 51, "High in the Tree"; sentence strips; pictures of trees and their fruits and nuts; *Henny Penny*; drawing materials	**Poem:** "I Had a Little Nut Tree" **Discussion and Shared Writing:** Dramatic Retelling of *Henny Penny* **Materials:** *Mighty Minutes* 56, "I Had a Little Nut Tree"; *Henny Penny*; story props; *Intentional Teaching Card* LL06, "Dramatic Story Retelling"	
Trees Count	*Chicka Chicka Boom Boom*	
Option 1: Same Sound Sort *Intentional Teaching Card* LL12, "Same Sound Sort"; a variety of small objects, some with the initial consonant /t/ sound; bag or box **Option 2: Tongue Twisters** *Intentional Teaching Card* LL16, "Tongue Twisters"	**Option 1: Alphabet Cards** *Intentional Teaching Card* LL03, "Alphabet Cards"; alphabet cards; small manipulatives **Option 2: Jumping Beans** *Intentional Teaching Card* LL05, "Jumping Beans"; construction paper; marker; scissors; lamination supplies or contact paper; coffee can	
Mighty Minutes 21, "Hully Gully, How Many?"; small tree parts	*Mighty Minutes* 10, "Words in Motion"	

Outdoor Experiences

Leaf Silhouettes

- Help children attach leaves to construction paper (any color but white) by using a small piece of clear tape. Try to use leaves with stems, and secure them to the paper by the stem.
- Put the papers in direct sunlight for a few days.
- Carefully check under the leaves each day. Point out the difference between the color underneath the leaves and the color of the paper around them, i.e., exposed to the sunlight.
- After a few days, remove each leaf to see its silhouette.
- Explain that energy from the sun helps trees and other living things grow and that the sun's energy changed the color of the paper.

Physical Fun

- Use *Intentional Teaching Card* P14, "Moving Through the Forest." Follow the guidance on the card

Family Partnerships

- Invite a family or community member to help make applesauce or apple bread with the children during small-group time on Day 3.
- Invite a family or community member to visit the classroom during Investigation 4, "Who cares for trees?" to talk about how to care for trees. A forester, arborist, or nursery worker is best. Call your local forest or parks department, tree care company, or garden center to locate an expert.
- Invite families to access the eBooks, *Who Lives in Trees?* and *Henny Penny*.

Wow! Experiences

- Day 3: Visit from someone who either grows food on trees or works with tree-grown food

What food comes from trees?

Vocabulary

English: See *Book Discussion Card* 15, *Henny Penny*, *(Pollita Pequeñita)*, for words.

Question of the Day: Did this grow on a tree? (Display a fruit or nut from a tree.)

Large Group

Opening Routine

- Sing a welcome song and talk about who's here.

Game: Hippity, Hoppity, How Many?

- Use *Mighty Minutes* 07, "Hippity, Hoppity, How Many?" Follow the guidance on the card.

Discussion and Shared Writing: Why Do Animals Live in Trees?

- Explain, "We've learned a lot about insects and other animals that live in trees." Remind the children of some of their discoveries.

- Ask, "Why do animals live in trees?"

- Explain, "Do you remember when the ladybug helped the tree by eating the aphids that were on the leaves? Trees are helpful to animals, too. Many animals depend on trees for food."

- Ask, "What kinds of foods grow on trees that insects and other animals eat?" (Responses might include leaves, small insects, fruit, seeds, and nuts.)

- Record the children's responses.

- Review the question of the day. Ask, "Is this a food that an insect or other animal might eat? Should we add it to the chart?" Save the chart for tomorrow's large-group discussion and read-aloud.

Before transitioning to interest areas, talk about the books in the Library area and how children can use them to find out what foods animals get from trees.

Choice Time

As you interact with children in the interest areas, make time to do the following:

- Help children find information in books by looking at the pictures.

- Read aloud the relevant parts of the books that explain the pictures.

> **Looking at books together to find answers to questions helps children learn that books can be a source of information.**

Read-Aloud

Read *Henny Penny*.

- Use *Book Discussion Card* 15, *Henny Penny.* Follow the guidance on the card for the second read-aloud.

Small Group

Option 1: I Went Shopping

- Use *Intentional Teaching Card* LL31, "I Went Shopping." Follow the guidance on the card.

Option 2: What's for Snack?

- Use *Intentional Teaching Card* LL25, "What's for Snack?" Follow the guidance on the card.

Understanding that print is meaningful is one of the first steps children take in learning to read and write. By drawing children's attention to the features of print, you help them understand print concepts, e.g., spoken words can be written, the direction in which words are written and read, there are spaces between words, and punctuation is used to end a sentence. See Objective 17: Demonstrates knowledge of print and its uses in *The Creative Curriculum® for Preschool, Volume 6:* Objectives for Development & Learning: Birth Through Kindergarten.

Mighty Minutes®

- Use *Mighty Minutes* 44, "Two Plump Armadillos." Follow the guidance on the card.

Large-Group Roundup

- Recall the day's events.
- Invite children who explored books about animals that eat foods from trees to share their discoveries.

What food comes from trees?

Vocabulary

English: *weigh, scale, heavier, lighter*

Spanish: *pesa, báscula, más pesado, más liviano*

Question of the Day: Did this grow on a tree? (Display a different fruit or nut from a tree.)

Large Group

Opening Routine

- Sing a welcome song and talk about who's here.

Rhyme: "High in the Tree"

- Use *Mighty Minutes* 51, "High in the Tree." Follow the guidance on the card.

Discussion and Shared Writing: Food Grown on Trees

- Remind children about the list they helped you create yesterday of tree-grown foods eaten by creatures that live in trees.

- Review the question of the day.

- Say, "Let's read this list together. As we read each food, tell me if it is one that people eat, too. If people eat it, show me a thumbs-up sign. If it is a food that people do not eat, show me a thumbs-down sign."

- Circle the items that the children agree are foods that people eat, too.

- Ask, "Do we eat other foods that grow on trees?"

Before transitioning to interest areas, talk about the scale in the Discovery area and using it to weigh tree parts.

Choice Time

As you interact with children in the interest areas, make time to do the following:

- Observe them exploring the tree parts and scale.

- Ask questions to encourage them to compare measurements, e.g., "Which orange is *heavier*?"

- Invite them to make predictions and then test them, e.g., "Which do you think will *weigh* more: the pinecone or five sticks?" "How many more sticks do you think you need to add to make the sides weigh the same?"

Read-Aloud

Read *Who Lives in Trees?*

- **Before you read**, ask, "Who remembers the name of this book?"

- **As you read**, pause and invite the children to say the repetitive line in the story.

- **After you read**, talk about the animals in the book that might eat food from the trees they live in. Refer back to the list you used during large-group time. Tell the children that the book will be available on the computer in the Technology area.

Small Group

Option 1: Nonsense Names

- Use *Intentional Teaching Card* LL10, "Rhyming Chart."

- Recall with the children the rhyming names in *Henny Penny*. Record them on a chart.

- Follow the guidance on the card. Use the children's names to create rhyming nonsense names.

Option 2: Rhyming Riddles

- Use *Intentional Teaching Card* LL11, "Rhyming Riddles." Follow the guidance on the card.

Mighty Minutes®

- Use *Mighty Minutes* 10, "Words in Motion." Follow the guidance on the card.

Large-Group Roundup

- Recall the day's events.

- Remind the children that someone who grows food on trees or who works with food grown on trees will be coming to the classroom tomorrow.

- Ask, "What questions would you like to ask our visitor?"

- Record their questions on a chart.

Investigation 3

What food comes from trees?

Vocabulary

English: *See Book Discussion Card 15, Henny Penny,*
(Pollita Pequeñita), for words.
Question of the Day: Did this grow on a tree? (Display an apple.)

Large Group

Opening Routine

- Sing a welcome song and talk about who's here.

Song: Strolling Through the Park

- Use *Mighty Minutes* 46, "Strolling Through the Park." Follow the guidance on the card.

Discussion and Shared Writing: Visitor Who Grows Food on Trees

- Introduce the visitor who grows food on trees or who works with tree-grown food.

- Invite the visitor to talk about his or her job.

- Invite the children to ask their questions from yesterday's large-group roundup.

- Record the visitor's answers.

- After the visitor has shared information with the children, pass around samples of food grown on trees for the children to examine and taste.

Before transitioning to interest areas, talk about the collage materials in the Art area and how children can use them.

Choice Time

As you interact with children in the interest areas, make time to do the following:

- Observe them as they work with the collage materials in the Art area.

- Invite them to talk about their collages.

Instead of praising children by saying "good job," encourage children by explaining exactly what they are doing that is appropriate and noteworthy. See *Intentional Teaching Card* SE18, "Encouragement," for ideas.

Read-Aloud

Read *Henny Penny*.

- Use *Book Discussion Card* 15, *Henny Penny.* Follow the guidance on the card for the third read-aloud.

- Tell the children that the book will be available on the computer in the Technology area.

Small Group

Option 1: Applesauce

- Use *Intentional Teaching Card* M28, "Applesauce." Follow the guidance on the card.

- Remind children that apples come from trees.

Option 2: Apple Bread

Review *Intentional Teaching Card* M29, "Apple Bread." Follow the guidance on the card.

English-Language Learners
Invite English-language learners' family members to help the children follow the recipes. The visitors can speak their first languages during the activity, thereby supporting children's confidence, comfort, and content learning. Meanwhile, other children will experience what English-language learners typically experience: trying to participate in an activity presented in a language they do not understand well.

Mighty Minutes®

- Use *Mighty Minutes* 04, "Riddle Dee Dee." Follow the guidance on the card. Use words about trees.

Large-Group Roundup

- Recall the day's events.

- Invite the children to write a group thank-you note to today's visitor.

English-Language Learners
When an English-language learner's family member visits to help with an activity, write the thank-you note in the first language and in English. Read the note with the children. Doing so supports bilingual learning for all children. If necessary, ask a family member or colleague to help with the first-language version. Encouraging families to continue talking to their children in their first languages supports dual-language learning. Children who have strong skills in their first languages typically do better in school than children with less proficiency.

What food comes from trees?

Vocabulary

English: *acorn*

Spanish: *bellota*

Question of the Day: Is *Henny Penny* a real story or pretend?

Large Group

Opening Routine

• Sing a welcome song and talk about who's here.

Rhyme: High in the Tree

• Use *Mighty Minutes* 51, "High in the Tree." Follow the guidance on the card.

Discussion and Shared Writing: *Henny Penny*

• Review the question of the day.

• Show the book *Henny Penny*. Remind the children about the *acorn* that fell on Henny Penny's head. Explain, "An *acorn* is a nut that many animals eat. It comes from an oak tree."

• Remind children about the silly names in the story.

• Say, "Let's add other animals to the story. Then you can tell me what we should name them."

• Ask, "What if there were a monkey in the story? What would her name be?"

• If children need help, suggest a silly rhyming name, such as *Funky Monkey*.

• Continue with other animal names. Record the children's funny names on a chart.

• Give the children some drawing materials and encourage them to draw a picture of one of the silly new characters they made up for the story.

> When children create silly names for the animals, they are using phonemic awareness skills. With *Funky Monkey*, they are substituting the initial consonant sound, or onset, with a new initial sound.

Before transitioning to interest areas, invite children who would like to continue working on their illustrations to take their materials to the Art area.

Choice Time	As you interact with children in the interest areas, make time to do the following: • Talk with the children about their illustrations as they draw in the Art area.	• Invite them to label their pictures with the silly, rhyming animal names.

Read-Aloud

Read *Trees Count*.

• **Before you read**, say, "We've read this book before. Let's read it again and see if we can find out anything new about the kinds of foods that grow on trees."

• **As you read**, point out the foods on the tree. Add them to the list of tree-grown foods that you started on Day 1 of this investigation.

• **After you read**, explain, "Each page illustrates a number by showing an amount. This one (show the page with the pecan tree) shows three branches." Invite children to make their own tree counting book. Encourage them to pick a number to represent something about a tree, e.g., "Ari, you picked the number *six*. What will you draw six times on your tree?" Tell the children that the book will be available on the computer in the Technology area.

Small Group

Option 1: Same Sound Sort

• Use *Intentional Teaching Card* LL12, "Same Sound Sort."

• Follow the guidance on the card. Use the /t/ sound.

English-Language Learners
When introducing English language sounds, begin with those common to both English and English-language learners' first languages.

Option 2: Tongue Twisters

• Use *Intentional Teaching Card* LL16, "Tongue Twisters."

• Follow the guidance on the card. Use the following tongue twister:

Ten tender, tangy tomatoes taste terrific on my tongue.

Alliterative tongue twisters help children focus on the initial sound of syllables and words.

Mighty Minutes®

• Use *Mighty Minutes* 21, "Hully Gully, How Many?" Follow the guidance on the card.

Large-Group Roundup

• Recall the day's events.

• Invite children to share their illustrations of new *Henny Penny* characters.

• Ask, "If we wanted to act out *Henny Penny*, what would help us tell the story?"

• Record their responses.

Day 5 | Investigation 3

What food comes from trees?

Vocabulary

English: *stretch, reach, lean, twist, flip, slide, roll*

Spanish: *estirarse, alcanzar, apoyarse, torcer, voltear, deslizar, rodar*

Question of the Day: Which food tastes best to you? (Offer samples of two tree-grown foods.)

Large Group

Opening Routine

- Sing a welcome song and talk about who's here.

Poem: "I Had a Little Nut Tree"

- Review the question of the day.

- Use *Mighty Minutes* 56, "I Had a Little Nut Tree." Follow the guidance on the card.

Discussion and Shared Writing: Dramatic Retelling of *Henny Penny*

- Invite children to retell the story of *Henny Penny*.

- Invite them to use the props they listed yesterday during large-group roundup as they tell the story.

> See *Intentional Teaching Card* LL06, "Dramatic Story Retelling," for more information.

Before transitioning to interest areas, tell the children that the props for *Henny Penny* will be available for them to use in the Dramatic Play area, and that the book will be available on the computer in the Technology area.

Choice Time

As you interact with children in the interest areas, make time to do the following:

- Observe children as they retell the story.

- Offer open-ended prompts to help children retell the story, e.g., "What happened next?"

- Comment on how children sequence the story and talk about the characters and events. "You put the story in a different sequence. You have Henny Penny meeting Foxy Loxy in the beginning of the story."

Read-Aloud

Read *Chicka Chicka Boom Boom*.

- **Before you read**, ask, "Who remembers the name of this book?"
- **As you read**, pause and encourage children to fill in many of the rhyming words and letters.

- **After you read**, look at the pages that show the letters after they have fallen out of the tree. Talk about the details of the pictures. Invite children to identify the letters.

Small Group

Option 1: Alphabet Cards

- Review *Intentional Teaching Card* LL03, "Alphabet Cards." Follow the guidance on the card.

Option 2: Jumping Beans

- Review *Intentional Teaching Card* LL05, "Jumping Beans." Follow the guidance on the card.

Mighty Minutes®

- Use *Mighty Minutes* 10, "Words in Motion." Follow the guidance on the card.

Large-Group Roundup

- Recall the day's events.
- Invite children who used props in the Dramatic Play area to demonstrate how they used them.

Investigation 4

Who takes care of trees?

Vocabulary—English: *national forest, forester, nursery worker, arborist, trunk, roots, crown, nutrients*

	Day 1	Day 2	Day 3
Interest Areas	**Art:** materials to make class books **Technology:** eBook version of *Growing Trees*	**Art:** materials to make class books	**Art:** materials to make class books **Technology:** eBook version of *Growing Trees*
Question of the Day	Which of these people takes care of trees? (Display, for example, a photo of a forester or arborist and one of a doctor.)	What would you like to ask our visitor today?	What did you learn from our visitor yesterday?
Large Group	**Rhyme:** "Two Plump Armadillos" **Discussion and Shared Writing:** Taking Care of Us and Taking Care of Trees **Materials:** *Mighty Minutes* 44, "Two Plump Armadillos"	**Poem:** "High in the Tree" **Discussion and Shared Writing:** Visitor Who Takes Care of Trees **Materials:** *Mighty Minutes* 51, "High in the Tree"; sentence strips with visual cues	**Game:** Echo Clapping **Discussion and Shared Writing:** Recalling the Tree Expert **Materials:** *Mighty Minutes* 26, "Echo Clapping"; rhythm sticks or drum; *Growing Trees*
Read-Aloud	*Growing Trees*	*Charlie Anderson*	*Growing Trees*
Small Group	**Option 1: Knowing Our Friends** *Intentional Teaching Card* LL30, "Knowing Our Friends"; children's name cards; feltboard or tagboard; large paper clip or hook-and-loop fastener **Option 2: Making My Name** *Intentional Teaching Card* LL29, "Making My Name"; small, sturdy envelopes; letter manipulatives	**Option 1: How Big Around?** *Intentional Teaching Card* M62, "How Big Around?"; several spherical objects; ball of yarn or string; scissors **Option 2: Measuring Tree Trunks** *Intentional Teaching Card* M62, "How Big Around?"; outdoor space; ball of yarn or string; scissors	**Option 1: Play Dough** *Intentional Teaching Card* M15, "Play Dough" (See card for equipment, recipe, and ingredients.) **Option 2: Peach Cobbler** *Intentional Teaching Card* M27, "Peach Cobbler" (See card for equipment, ingredients, and recipe.); *Gathering the Sun*
Mighty Minutes®	*Mighty Minutes* 52, "Walk Around the Shapes"; shape cards	*Mighty Minutes* 33, "Thumbs Up"	*Mighty Minutes* 33, "Thumbs Up"

Day 4	Make Time for…

Art: materials to make class books

Cooking: *Intentional Teaching Card* LL24, "Lemonade" (See card for equipment, ingredients, and recipe.)

Which food will help us be healthy and strong? (Display separate pictures of a *healthy* food and an *unhealthy* food.)

Poem: "High in the Tree"

Discussion and Shared Writing: Planting a Tree

Materials: *Mighty Minutes* 51, "High in the Tree"; sentence strips with visual cues; *Growing Trees*; small tree; materials for transplanting, e.g., larger pot, tree soil, trowels, watering can; or for planting tree outside, e.g., shovels, tree stakes, string, hose

Our Tree Named Steve

Option 1: Patterns in Trees

Intentional Teaching Card M14, "Patterns"; tree cookies (cross sections revealing the rings); drawing materials

Option 2: Photographing Patterns

Intentional Teaching Card M14, "Patterns"; outdoor space; digital camera; computer; drawing materials

Mighty Minutes 26, "Echo Clapping"

Outdoor Experiences

Physical Fun

- Use *Intentional Teaching Card* P13, "Punting." Follow the guidance on the card.

Family Partnerships

- Invite a family member to visit the class and cook with the children on Day 3 of this investigation.

- Invite families to access the eBook, *Growing Trees*.

Wow! Experiences

- Day 2: A visit from someone who takes care of trees

Day 1 Investigation 4

Who takes care of trees?

Vocabulary

English: *national forest, forester, nursery worker, arborist*

Spanish: *bosque nacional, guardabosques, empleado*(a) de un invernadero, especialista en árboles

Question of the Day: Which of these people takes care of trees? (Display, for example, a photo of a forester or arborist and one of a doctor.)

Large Group

Opening Routine

- Sing a welcome song and talk about who's here.

Rhyme: "Two Plump Armadillos"

- Use *Mighty Minutes* 44, "Two Plump Armadillos." Follow the guidance on the card.

Discussion and Shared Writing: Taking Care of Us and Taking Care of Trees

- Prepare a chart with two columns. Label them "Who takes care of us?" and "Who takes care of trees?"

- Say, "Even the armadillo has someone to take care of him: his dad."

- Ask, "Who takes care of us?" Record the children's responses in the appropriate column on the chart.

- Ask, "What tools do these people use to take care of us?" If the children need help, suggest that a mother might use a thermometer when a child is sick and that a doctor uses a stethoscope to listen to hearts. Record the children's responses.

- Say, "I wonder who takes care of trees. I wonder what kinds of tools those people use to care for the trees."

Before transitioning to interest areas, talk about the bookmaking materials in the Art area. Discuss how the children can use them to illustrate pages for a class book.

Choice Time

As you interact with children in the interest areas, make time to do the following:

- Ask children to imagine seeing something in a tree. Prompt their ideas with the following refrain: [*Gracie, Gracie*] *what do you see? I see a* [*monkey*] *in my tree.*

- Assist them in writing the adapted refrains as the captions for their illustrations. Invite them to write their names and any other words or letters that they can write.

- Save the pages, and add them to other pages the children will make for a class book.

English-Language Learners
To include children who are not yet speaking much English in a discussion, hold up pictures of things one might see in a tree. Invite them to point to the items as they are named. Alternatively, include answer options in the phrasing of the question. For example, ask, "Which animal might you see in a tree: a bird or a fish?"

Read-Aloud

Read *Growing Trees*.

- **Before you read**, remind children about the "Who takes care of trees?" question from large-group time. Show the cover, and read the title of the story. Say, "I wonder whether we'll find an answer to our question in this book. Let's read it to find out."

- **As you read**, explain the following terms: *national forest*, *forester*, *nursery worker*, and *arborist*.

- **After you read**, refer to your chart from large-group time. Ask, "What did this book tell us about who takes care of trees and the tools they use?" Record children's ideas on the chart. Tell the children that the book will be available on the computer in the Technology area.

Small Group

Option 1: Knowing Our Friends

- Review *Intentional Teaching Card* LL30, "Knowing Our Friends." Follow the guidance on the card.

Option 2: Making My Name

- Review *Intentional Teaching Card* LL29, "Making My Name." Follow the guidance on the card.

Mighty Minutes®

- Use *Mighty Minutes* 52, "Walk Around the Shapes." Follow the guidance on the card.

Large-Group Roundup

- Recall the day's events.
- Remind children that someone who takes care of trees will be visiting the class tomorrow.

- Ask, "What would you like to ask our visitor tomorrow?" Record the children's questions.

Day 2   Investigation 4

Who takes care of trees?

Vocabulary

English: See *Book Discussion Card* 17, *Charlie Anderson, for words.*
Question of the Day: What would you like to ask our visitor today?

Large Group

Opening Routine

- Sing a welcome song and talk about who's here.

Poem: "High in the Tree"

- Use *Mighty Minutes* 51, "High in the Tree." Follow the guidance on the card.

Discussion and Shared Writing: Visitor Who Takes Care of Trees

- Introduce the visitor who takes care of trees.

- Ask the visitor to talk about his or her job and the tools involved in it.

- Invite the children to ask their questions from yesterday's large-group roundup and from the question of the day.

- Record the visitor's responses.

Before transitioning to interest areas, talk about the bookmaking materials in the Art area. Discuss how the children can use them to illustrate pages for a class book.

Choice Time

As you interact with children in the interest areas, make time to do the following:

- Ask children to imagine seeing something in a tree. Prompt their ideas with the following refrain: [*Gracie, Gracie*] *what do you see? I see a* [*monkey*] *in my tree.*

- Assist them in writing the adapted refrains as captions for their illustrations. Invite them to write their names and any other words or letters that they can.

- Save the pages throughout the week and add them to a class book.

> **Working on a class book or another whole-group project helps children build a sense of classroom community.**

Read-Aloud

Read *Charlie Anderson*.

- **Before you read**, show the cover of the book and read the title.

- **As you read**, pause occasionally, inviting children to comment on the events of the story.

- **After you read**, talk about Charlie Anderson's experience walking through the woods. Ask, "What do you think it was like for Charlie to walk through the woods? How do you think he felt? What other animals do you think he met along the way?"

Small Group

Option 1: How Big Around?

- Use *Intentional Teaching Card* M62, "How Big Around?"

- Follow the guidance on the card. Have the children measure the circumference of several large tree parts from the collection. Assist them, as needed.

Option 2: Measuring Tree Trunks

- Use *Intentional Teaching Card* M62, "How Big Around?"

- Take the children outdoors. Follow the guidance on the card to measure the circumference of trees on the playground.

Mighty Minutes®

- Use *Mighty Minutes* 33, "Thumbs Up." Follow the guidance on the card.

Large-Group Roundup

- Recall the day's events.

- Write a group thank-you note to today's visitor. Invite the children to add drawings to the note and sign their names.

Day 3 | Investigation 4

Who takes care of trees?

Vocabulary

English: *forester, nursery worker, arborist*

Spanish: *guardabosques, empleado*(a) de un invernadero, especialista en árboles

Question of the Day: What did you learn from our visitor yesterday?

Large Group

Opening Routine

- Sing a welcome song and talk about who's here.

Game: Echo Clapping

- Use *Mighty Minutes* 26, "Echo Clapping." Follow the guidance on the card.

English-Language Learners

Echo clapping helps children build phonological memory skills. The ability to remember language sounds is a strong predictor of later literacy development.

Discussion and Shared Writing: Recalling the Tree Expert

- Recall with the children yesterday's visit from a tree expert.
- Tell something you learned from the expert.
- Ask the question of the day.
- Record the children's responses.
- Ask, "What do trees need to be healthy and strong?"
- Record the children's responses.
- If the visitor didn't answer that question yesterday, use *Growing Trees* to help children find the information.

Before transitioning to interest areas, talk about the bookmaking materials in the Art area. Discuss how the children can use them to illustrate pages for a class book.

Choice Time	As you interact with children in the interest areas, make time to do the following: • Ask children to imagine seeing something in a tree. Prompt their ideas with the following refrain: [*Gracie, Gracie*] *what do you see? I see a* [*monkey*] *in my tree.*	• Assist them in writing the adapted refrains as the captions for their illustrations. Encourage them to write their names and any other words or letters that they can write. • Save the pages to add to those the children worked on throughout the week for a class book.
Read-Aloud	Read *Growing Trees*. • **Before you read**, ask, "What do you remember about this book?" • **As you read**, point out interesting details in the pictures and reinforce the words *forester*, *nursery worker*, and *arborist*.	• **After you read**, talk about the similarities between what the visitor said about caring for trees and what the book says about tree care.

	Option 1: Play Dough	**Option 2: Peach Cobbler**
Small Group	• Use *Intentional Teaching Card* M15, "Play Dough." Follow the guidance on the card.	• Use *Intentional Teaching Card* M27, "Peach Cobbler." Follow the guidance on the card. Read children the poem, "Duraznos/Peaches" in *Gathering the Sun*. Talk about the illustration, e.g., peach trees, peach orchard, farmworkers on ladders picking fruit.

Mighty Minutes®	• Use *Mighty Minutes* 33, "Thumbs Up." Try the alliterative variation on the back of the card.	**English-Language Learners** English-language learners may have difficulty with alliterative activities based on sounds that are not part of their first languages or sounds with a different function. If that is the case, base the activity on an initial consonant sound that all of the children in your class can distinguish and pronounce easily.
Large-Group Roundup	• Recall the day's events. • Invite children who worked on book pages in the Art area to share their work.	

Who takes care of trees?

Vocabulary

English: *trunk, roots, crown, nutrients*

Spanish: *tronco, raíces, copa, nutrientes*

Question of the Day: Which food will help us be healthy and strong? (Display separate pictures of a healthy food and an *unhealthy* food.)

Large Group

Opening Routine

- Sing a welcome song and talk about who's here.

Poem: "High in the Tree"

- Use *Mighty Minutes* 51, "High in the Tree." Follow the guidance on the card.

Discussion and Shared Writing: Planting a Tree

- Remind children how the girl in *Growing Trees* planted her tree.

- Say, "Today, I need your help to plant a tree of our own."

- With the children's help, transplant a small tree to a larger pot or plant a tree outdoors.

- Talk about the parts of the tree as you plant it, e.g., the *trunk, roots,* and *crown.*

Remind children about the jobs each different tree part performs. Say, for example, "The *roots* go deep into the ground. They hold the tree steady. They also get water and *nutrients* from the soil to help the tree grow."

- Ask, "How should we care for our tree?"

- Record the children's responses.

> **Contact your local forestry office or the Arbor Day Foundation for details on getting free trees.**

Before transitioning to interest areas, talk about the bookmaking materials in the Art area. Discuss their use for illustrating pages for a class book. Also explain the recipe found in *Come Cook With Me* and ingredients for making lemonade in the Cooking area.

Choice Time

As you interact with children in the interest areas, make time to do the following:

- Ask children to imagine seeing something in a tree. Prompt their ideas with the following refrain: [*Gracie, Gracie*] *what do you see? I see a* [*monkey*] *in my tree.*

- Assist them in writing the adapted refrains as the captions for their illustrations. Invite them to write their names and any other words or letters they can write.

- Have children help you bind the illustrated pages as a class book.

- Help the children make lemonade in the Cooking area. Invite them to do as much of the activity as possible by themselves, including reading the recipe chart. See *Intentional Teaching Card* LL24, "Lemonade."

Read-Aloud	Read *Our Tree Named Steve*. • **Before you read**, ask, "What is the name of this book?"	• **As you read**, talk about what the family did to care for the tree. • **After you read**, vote on a name for the class tree.

Small Group

Option 1: Patterns in Trees

• Use *Intentional Teaching Card* M14, "Patterns."

• Invite children to look closely at a few tree cookies (cross sections revealing the rings). Talk about what they notice. Point out the ring pattern.

• Follow the guidance on the card. Have children draw patterns inspired by their investigation of the tree cookies.

Option 2: Photographing Patterns

• Use *Intentional Teaching Card* M14, "Patterns." Follow the guidance on the card.

• Take the children outside for a close look at a nearby tree.

• Invite children to look for patterns in the tree, e.g., bark with alternating dark and light lines or a flower with a pink line and yellow dot on every petal.

• Invite the children to photograph the patterns they see.

• Return to the classroom to view and print the photos.

Children may ask questions that stump you. For example, a child might ask, "Why are some rings dark and some rings light?" (In North America, light rings grow during late spring and early summer, and dark rings form later in the summer and during early fall.) "Why are some rings thick and some rings thin?" (Thin rings show drought years.) When you are uncertain of the answers, help children find them in books or on the Internet.

Mighty Minutes®

• Use *Mighty Minutes* 26, "Echo Clapping." Follow the guidance on the card.

Large-Group Roundup

• Recall the day's events.

• Invite children to share the patterns they discovered in the trees or tree cookies that they examined today.

• Share the class book. Invite children to read their refrains and describe their illustrations.

Investigation 5

How do trees change?

Vocabulary—English: *adult, inspiration, seed, seedling, sapling, imagine, damage*

	Day 1	Day 2	Day 3
Interest Areas	**Art:** landscape painting for inspiration at the easel; *Colors! ¡Colores!*	**Art:** landscape painting for inspiration at the easel **Technology:** eBook versions of *Growing Trees* and *Trees, Trees, Trees*	**Library:** writing materials; *Intentional Teaching Card* LL27, "Writing Poems"; audio recorder
Question of the Day	How tall were you when you were a baby? (Have the children put pieces of masking tape on the wall with their names on them to mark their answer. Save these markings for future comparisons.)	How tall are you now? (Have the children mark their current heights with masking tape next to their estimates from yesterday.)	Is this a living or nonliving thing? (Display an item from the classroom.)
Large Group	**Movement:** Counting Calisthenics **Discussion and Shared Writing:** We Grow, and Trees Grow **Materials:** *Mighty Minutes* 28, "Counting Calisthenics"; masking tape; picture of yourself as a baby; lifelike baby doll; cardboard blocks; digital camera	**Rhyme:** "Come Play With Me" **Discussion and Shared Writing:** Seed, Seedling, and Sapling **Materials:** *Mighty Minutes* 42, "Come Play With Me"; *Trees, Trees, Trees*; masking tape	**Movement:** Counting Calisthenics **Discussion and Shared Writing:** Living and Nonliving Things **Materials:** *Mighty Minutes* 28, "Counting Calisthenics"; *Intentional Teaching Card* LL58, "Our Super-Duper Writing Box"
Read-Aloud	*When the Monkeys Came Back* *Intentional Teaching Card* SE05, "Character Feelings"	*Growing Trees*	*When the Monkeys Came Back* *Intentional Teaching Card* LL06, "Dramatic Story Retelling"
Small Group	**Option 1: Shapes, Shapes, Shapes** *Intentional Teaching Card* M21, "Geoboards"; geoboards; rubber bands; shape cards **Option 2: The Busy Farmer** *Intentional Teaching Card* M50, "The Farmer Builds a Fence"; large elastic band; two-dimensional shapes	**Option 1: Letters, Letters, Letters** *Intentional Teaching Card* LL07, "Letters, Letters, Letters"; alphabet stamps; colored inkpads; construction paper **Option 2: Shaving Cream Letters** *Intentional Teaching Card* LL13, "Shaving Cream Letters"; shaving creams	**Option 1: Which Has More?** *Intentional Teaching Card* M19, "Which Has More?"; ice cube trays or egg cartons; resealable bags; collection of similarly sized objects **Option 2: Dinnertime** *Intentional Teaching Card* M01, "Dinnertime"; paper or plastic dishes; utensils; napkins; cups; placemats
Mighty Minutes®	*Mighty Minutes* 08, "Clap the Missing Word"	*Mighty Minutes* 57, "Find the Letter Sound"; letter cards	*Mighty Minutes* 24, "Dinky Doo"

Day 4	Day 5	Make Time for...
Art: paints; colorful leaves **Library:** *Who Lives in Trees?* **Technology:** eBook version of *Who Lives in Trees?*	**Technology:** eBook version of *Trees, Trees, Trees; Intentional Teaching Card* LL02, "Desktop Publishing"; digital camera; printer; each child's word bank; bookbinding supplies	## Outdoor Experiences **Squirrels in Trees** • Invite children to pretend to be squirrels playing in the trees. • Use positional words to tell the "squirrels" where to run next, e.g., behind the tree, in front of the tree, or next to the tree.
What two colors can we mix together to make this color? (Display a sample of orange paint.)	What do you think happened to this tree? (Display a picture of a damaged tree.)	## Family Partnerships • Invite families to participate in the celebration at the end of this study. • Invite a family or community member who makes things from wood to visit the classroom during Investigation 6, "What can we do with parts of trees?" This person might be a carpenter, a construction worker, a furniture maker, or someone who assembles wooden furniture in a furniture store. Invite the visitor to demonstrate how he or she builds with wood and talk about the tools that are required for furniture making.
Movement: Riddle Dee Dee **Discussion and Shared Writing:** Tree Poems **Materials:** *Mighty Minutes* 04, "Riddle Dee Dee"; several tree poems by children; *Mighty Minutes* 49, "A Tree My Size"; paper and pencils	**Game:** Clap the Beat **Discussion and Shared Writing:** Tree Damage **Materials:** *Mighty Minutes* 59, "Clap the Beat"; collection of tree parts; drums or rhythm sticks; *Growing Trees; Who Lives in Trees?*	
Pablo's Tree; chart paper; markers	*Trees, Trees, Trees Intentional Teaching Card* LL26, "Searching the Web"	
Option 1: Dramatic Story Retelling *Intentional Teaching Card* LL06, "Dramatic Story Retelling"; *Henny Penny;* story props **Option 2: Clothesline Storytelling** *Intentional Teaching Card* LL33, "Clothesline Storytelling"; *Henny Penny;* lamination supplies; 6 ft of clothesline and clothespins; a paper star; large resealable bag	**Option 1: Dramatic Story Retelling** *Intentional Teaching Card* LL06, "Dramatic Story Retelling"; *Henny Penny;* story props **Option 2: Clothesline Storytelling** *Intentional Teaching Card* LL33, "Clothesline Storytelling"; *Henny Penny;* lamination supplies; 6 ft of clothesline and clothespins; a paper star; large resealable bag	
Mighty Minutes 15, "Say it, Show it"; numeral cards	*Mighty Minutes* 53, "Three Rowdy Children"; letter cards	

How do trees change?

Vocabulary

English: *adult, inspiration*

Spanish: *adulto, inspiración*

Question of the day: How tall were you when you were a baby? (Have the children put pieces of masking tape on the wall with their names on them to mark their answer. Save these markings for future comparisons.)

Large Group

Opening Routine

- Sing a welcome song and talk about who's here.

Movement: Counting Calisthenics

- Use *Mighty Minutes* 28, "Counting Calisthenics." Follow the guidance on the card.

Discussion and Shared Writing: We Grow and Trees Grow

- Show the children a picture of yourself as a baby.

- Explain, "I used to be a very small baby. I grew a little bigger every year. My body changed, and it grew taller. Now that I'm an *adult,* I've stopped growing taller."

- Use a lifelike baby doll to compare your height as a baby with your height as an adult. Invite the children to compare their heights with the doll's height.

- Review the question of the day.

- Ask, "How tall do you think you will be when you are an *adult*?"

- With the children's help, stack cardboard blocks or other large, lightweight building blocks to the height that individual children predict they will be. Take pictures of the children next to the stacked blocks.

- Explain, "When trees are planted and when they grow from seeds, they are very small. They grow taller every year, just as we do. We know from reading about trees and planting our tree that they need soil, sunlight, and water to grow. Growing taller is one way that trees change."

- Ask, "Can you think of other ways that trees change?" Record the children's responses. Save the chart for tomorrow's large-group discussion.

Before transitioning to interest areas, talk about the landscape painting in the Art area. Discuss how the children can use it as *inspiration* for their own artwork.

> **If you don't have a landscape painting, place an interesting tree artifact and *Colors! ¡Colores!* in the Art area to inspire children's art.**

Choice Time	As you interact with children in the interest areas, make time to do the following: • Talk to children about their artwork. • Ask them to explain how they created their art.	Hanging children's artwork among well-known reproductions shows them how much you value their art.

Read-Aloud	Read *When the Monkeys Came Back*. • **Before you read**, show the cover and ask, "Who can tell us what this book is about?" Read the title. • **As you read**, pause occasionally to point out the details in the illustrations.	• **After you read**, see *Intentional Teaching Card* SE05, "Character Feelings," to discuss Doña Marta's feelings at the end of the story.

Small Group	**Option 1: Shapes, Shapes, Shapes** • Use *Intentional Teaching Card* M21, "Geoboards." Follow the guidance on the card. Geoboards help children understand geometry, develop spatial skills, and develop mathematical thinking.	**Option 2: The Busy Farmer** • Use *Intentional Teaching Card* M50, "The Farmer Builds a Fence." Follow the guidance on the card.

Mighty Minutes®	• Use *Mighty Minutes* 08, "Clap the Missing Word." Follow the guidance on the card.

Large-Group Roundup	• Recall the day's events. • Invite children to share their artwork.

How do trees change?

Vocabulary

English: *seed, seedling, sapling*

Spanish: *semilla, plántula, árbol jóven*

Question of the Day: How tall are you now? (Have the children mark their current heights with masking tape next to their estimates from yesterday.)

Large Group

Opening Routine

- Sing a welcome song and talk about who's here.

Rhyme: "Come Play With Me"

- Use *Mighty Minutes* 42, "Come Play With Me." Follow the guidance on the card.

Discussion and Shared Writing: Seed, Seedling, and Sapling

- Read *Trees, Trees, Trees.* Talk about the words *seed, seedling,* and *sapling.*

- After reading, review the question of the day. Talk about how the children changed in height since they were babies.

- Review the chart from yesterday. Ask, "What other ways do trees change?"

- Record the children's responses.

- Explain, "Trees grow and change, just as we do. Trees need food and water, just like us. We are living things, and so are trees. Living things grow and change. Living things need food and water."

- Point out a few items around the classroom and ask, "Is [the goldfish] a living thing? Is this table alive? Is it a living thing? Why not?"

Before transitioning to interest areas, talk about the materials in the Art area. Discuss how the children can use them to create paintings or sculptures to add to the display about how trees change. Tell the children that the book will be available on the computer in the Technology area.

Choice Time

As you interact with children in the interest areas, make time to do the following:

- Talk to them about their artwork.

- On another piece of paper, record what they say about their artwork. Display their narratives next to their work.

English-Language Learners

Incorporate new vocabulary into as many classroom activities as possible and explain the words in your conversations with children. These strategies help all children learn new words.

Read-Aloud

Read *Growing Trees*.

• **Before you read**, ask, "Who remembers something about this book?"

• **As you read**, point out the pictures of changing trees.

• **After you read**, talk about the different ways in which the trees in the book changed. Tell the children that the book will be available on the computer in the Technology area.

Small Group

Option 1: Letters, Letters, Letters

• Use *Intentional Teaching Card* LL07, "Letters, Letters, Letters." Follow the guidance on the card.

Option 2: Shaving Cream Letters

• Use *Intentional Teaching Card* LL13, "Shaving Cream Letters." Follow the guidance on the card.

Mighty Minutes®

• Use *Mighty Minutes* 57, "Find the Letter Sound." Follow the guidance on the card.

> Young children's alphabet knowledge, especially their ability to rapidly name letters in random order, is a strong predictor of later reading, writing, and spelling ability. There is a high correlation between knowing names of the letters and knowing letter sounds.

Large-Group Roundup

• Recall the day's events.

• Review *Intentional Teaching Card* SE10, "My Turn at the Microphone," and invite children who created artwork for the tree display to share their work.

How do trees change?

Vocabulary

English: *living, nonliving*

Spanish: *vivo, no vivo* (inerte)

Question of the Day: Is this a living or nonliving thing? (Display an item from the classroom.)

Large Group

Opening Routine

- Sing a welcome song and talk about who's here.

Movement: Counting Calisthenics

- Use *Mighty Minutes* 28, "Counting Calisthenics." Follow the guidance on the card.

Discussion and Shared Writing: Living and Nonliving Things

- Remind children about yesterday's large-group discussion. Ask, "How can we tell whether something is living or nonliving?"

- Record their responses and add to them if necessary. Save the chart for the first large-group discussion in Investigation 6, "What can we do with the parts of trees?"

- Review the question of the day.

- Ask, "What are some other living things?" Refer back to their criteria for defining living things to check their responses. "Calvin says that the flowers on our playground are living. Do they need food and water? Do they grow?"

Before transitioning to interest areas, talk about the writing materials available in the Library area and how children can use them to write poems about trees.

> Sometimes children need something new to engage them in writing. See *Intentional Teaching Card* LL58, "Our Super-Duper Writing Box," for a playful idea.

Choice Time

As you interact with children in the interest areas, make time to do the following:

- Record the children reciting their poems in the Library area.

- Invite them to look at books about trees for inspiration.

> For more information about helping children write poems, see *Intentional Teaching Card* LL27, "Writing Poems."

English-Language Learners
Try to provide books and poetry collections written in children's first languages. These materials can help English-language learners participate more fully in poetry-related activities. A multilingual library also helps children understand that languages have different alphabets and representations, and are not always written and read from left to right.

Read-Aloud

Read *When the Monkeys Came Back*.

- Use *Intentional Teaching Card* LL06, "Dramatic Story Retelling," to encourage the children to act out the story.

Small Group

Option 1: Which Has More?

- Use *Intentional Teaching Card* M19, "Which Has More?" Follow the guidance on the card.

Option 2: Dinnertime

- Use *Intentional Teaching Card* M01, "Dinnertime." Follow the guidance on the card.

Mighty Minutes®

- Use *Mighty Minutes* 24, "Dinky Doo." Follow the guidance on the card.

Large-Group Roundup

- Recall the day's events.
- Invite children to share the poems they wrote about trees during choice time. Play some of the recordings you made of their recitations.

How do trees change?

Vocabulary

English: *imagine*

Spanish: *imaginar*

Question of the Day: What two colors can we mix together to make this color? (Display a sample of orange paint.)

Large Group

Opening Routine

- Sing a welcome song and talk about who's here.

Movement: Riddle Dee Dee

- Use *Mighty Minutes* 04, "Riddle Dee Dee."

- Try the "jump the syllables" variation on the back of the card.

Discussion and Shared Writing: Tree Poems

- Read some of the tree poems that children have written during the study.

- Explain, "I'm going to read a poem. I want you to close your eyes while I read. Think about the words I'm reading. Try to *imagine* what I'm describing. Make a picture of it in your mind."

- Read one of the children's poems or use *Mighty Minutes* 49, "A Tree My Size."

- After you read, ask the children to open their eyes and tell you what they imagined while you read.

- Read the poem again. After you read, give the children paper and pencils. Invite them to draw what they imagined as you read the poem.

> When you help children think about past, future, or fictitious events, you are using decontextualized language. Research shows that this type of talk by teachers is important for children's language and literacy development.

Before transitioning to interest areas, talk about the paints and leaves in the Art area. Discuss how the children can mix paints to match the colors they see in the leaves. Review the question of the day.

Choice Time

As you interact with children in the interest areas, make time to do the following:

- Observe them as they mix the paints in the Art area. Describe what you see, e.g., "Keiko, you mixed colors together to make dark brown."

- Ask questions that encourage children to explain processes. Say, for example, "Which colors did you use to make brown? Did you use more yellow or more black?"

- Read *Who Lives in Trees?* Talk about the colors of the leaves in the book. Remind the children that some trees change because they are harmed.

Read-Aloud

Read *Pablo's Tree.*

- **Before you read**, tell children the name of the book. Invite them to describe the illustration on the cover. Ask, "Why do you think Pablo has his own tree? Why are there decorations on it?"

- **As you read**, write on chart paper what Lito puts on Pablo's tree for each birthday. Point out that both the tree and Pablo get taller every year and that the tree eventually looks taller than Lito.

- **After you read**, ask, "What do you think Lito will put on Pablo's tree?"

Small Group

Option 1: Dramatic Story Retelling

- Use *Intentional Teaching Card* LL06, "Dramatic Story Retelling."

- Follow the guidance on the card. Use *Henny Penny.*

Option 2: Clothesline Storytelling

- Use *Intentional Teaching Card* LL33, "Clothesline Storytelling."

- Follow the guidance on the card. Use *Henny Penny.*

Story retelling helps preschoolers build comprehension skills.

Mighty Minutes®

- Use *Mighty Minutes* 15, "Say It, Show It." Follow the guidance on the card.

Large-Group Roundup

- Recall the day's events.

- Invite children who mixed paint in the Art area to share their work.

Investigation 5

How do trees change?

Vocabulary

English: *damage*

Spanish: *dañar*

Question of the Day: What do you think happened to this tree? (Display a picture of a damaged tree.)

Large Group

Opening Routine

- Sing a welcome song and talk about who's here.

Game: Clap the Beat

- Use *Mighty Minutes* 59, "Clap the Beat." Follow the guidance on the card.

Discussion and Shared Writing: Tree Damage

- Turn to the page in *Growing Trees* where the arborist cares for a tree that was damaged by bad weather.

- Explain, "Bad weather can *damage*, or hurt, trees."

- Review the question of the day.

- Ask, "What else can *damage* trees?" Record the children's responses.

- Remind children of the discussion you had a while ago about insects and other animals that harm trees.

- Display page 23 of *Who Lives in Trees?* Add items to the list of things that can damage trees.

Before transitioning to interest areas, explain to the children that they may work together to make a picture book of living and nonliving things in the classroom.

Choice Time

As you interact with children in the interest areas, make time to do the following:

- Invite children to take pictures of living and nonliving things in the classroom.

- Help them print their photos and assemble them to make a book.

> **See *Intentional Teaching Card* LL02, "Desktop Publishing," for more information.**

Read-Aloud

Read *Trees, Trees, Trees*.

- **Before you read**, remind the children of the useful information you found together in this book.

- **As you read**, invite children to add what they have learned about trees to the information found in the book.

- **After you read**, review the "What do we want to find out about trees?" chart. Point out the questions that you will be exploring in the next investigation and revisit previous questions. Help children research any unanswered questions on the Internet or in books. Tell the children that the book will be available on the computer in the Technology area.

> **For more information about helping children research their questions online, see *Intentional Teaching Card* LL26, "Searching the Web."**

Small Group

Option 1: Dramatic Story Retelling

- Use *Intentional Teaching Card* LL06, "Dramatic Story Retelling." Follow the guidance on the card using *Henny Penny*.

Option 2: Clothesline Storytelling

- Use *Intentional Teaching Card* LL33, "Clothesline Storytelling." Follow the guidance on the card using *Henny Penny.*

> **Research shows that children who frequently retell and act out stories tend to have better vocabularies and story comprehension, and use more complex language than children who only draw or talk generally about stories.**

Mighty Minutes®

- Use *Mighty Minutes* 53, "Three Rowdy Children." Follow the guidance on the card.

Large-Group Roundup

- Recall the day's events.

- Invite children who took pictures of living and nonliving things in the classroom today to share their favorites.

Investigation 6

What can we do with parts of trees?

Vocabulary—English: *wooden*

	Day 1	Day 2	Day 3
Interest Areas	**Discovery:** wood, sandpaper; digital camera **Technology:** eBook versions of *A Tree Is For...*	**Discovery:** variety of papers; magnifying glasses; *Intentional Teaching Card* LL63, "Investigating & Recording"	**Discovery:** wood, woodworking tools **Technology:** eBook versions of *A Tree Is For...*
Question of the Day	Are there more or fewer than 10 sticks in the guessing jar?	What would you like to ask our visitor today?	Is our school made from wood?
Large Group	**Music:** Drums **Discussion and Shared Writing:** What Things Are Made From Wood? **Materials:** guessing jar filled with sticks; drums; collection of tree parts and wooden and nonwooden objects	**Music:** Beating Drum Patterns **Discussion and Shared Writing:** Visitor Who Makes Things From Wood **Materials:** *Mighty Minutes* 26, "Echo Clapping"; drums	**Game:** 1, 2, 3, What Do I See? **Discussion and Shared Writing:** Woodworking Tools **Materials:** *Mighty Minutes* 50, "1, 2, 3, What Do I See?"; small basket of tree parts; scarf or other piece of fabric
Read-Aloud	*A Tree Is For...*	*A Grand Old Tree Book Discussion Card* 16 (first read-aloud)	*A Tree Is For...*
Small Group	**Option 1: Drawing a House** *Intentional Teaching Card* LL32, "Describing Art"; *The Three Little Pigs*; drawing supplies **Option 2: Building a House** *Intentional Teaching Card* LL32, "Describing Art"; *The Three Little Pigs*; straw; small sticks, twigs, or craft sticks; clay	**Option 1: Wooden Collections** *Intentional Teaching Card* M05, "Sorting & Classifying"; objects that define boundaries for sorting **Option 2: Wood Hunt** *Intentional Teaching Card* M05, "Sorting & Classifying"; digital camera; objects that define boundaries for sorting	**Option 1: A Closer Look at Wood** *Intentional Teaching Card* LL63, "Investigating & Recording"; magnifying glasses; collection of wooden objects; small clipboards; paper and pencils **Option 2: Close Up Outdoors** *Intentional Teaching Card* LL63, "Investigating & Recording"; magnifying glasses; outdoor space with trees and–or other wooden items; clipboards; paper and pencils
Mighty Minutes®	*Mighty Minutes* 20, "I Can Make a Circle"	*Mighty Minutes* 18, "I'm Thinking Of…"	*Mighty Minutes* 57, "Find the Letter Sound"; letter cards

Day 4	Make Time for…

Music and Movement: wooden instruments

Which wooden instrument would you like to play? (Display two or three different instruments.)

Music: Beating Drum Patterns

Discussion and Shared Writing: Exploring Wooden Instruments

Materials: *Mighty Minutes* 26, "Echo Clapping"; drums; collection of wooden instruments; audio recorder

A Grand Old Tree
Book Discussion Card 16
(second read-aloud)

Option 1: Tallying

Intentional Teaching Card M06, "Tallying"; clipboard; paper; pencils or crayons

Option 2: Graphing

Intentional Teaching Card M11, "Graphing"; large graph paper or lined chart paper; markers; stickers; pictures

Mighty Minutes 55, "Mr. Forgetful"

Outdoor Experiences

Physical Fun

- Use *Intentional Teaching Card* P14, "Moving Through the Forest." Follow the guidance on the card.

Family Partnerships

- Invite families to participate in the celebration at the end of this study.
- Invite families to access the eBooks, *A Tree Is For…* and *The Three Little Pigs*.

Wow! Experiences

- Day 2: A visit from a person who makes things out of wood

Invite the visitor to demonstrate how he or she makes something from wood.

85

What can we do with parts of trees?

Vocabulary

English: *wooden*

Spanish: *de madera*

Question of the Day: Are there more or fewer than 10 sticks in the guessing jar?

Large Group

Opening Routine

- Sing a welcome song and talk about who's here.

Music: Drums

- Use a real drum to demonstrate how a drum can be played, e.g., loudly and quietly, or quickly and slowly.

- Talk about the difference between just making noise and making music.

- Give each child a drum, or encourage the children to find things in the room that they can use as drums.

- Show them how to hold their drums in a resting position until everyone is ready.

- Play the beat to a familiar tune, and invite the children to play along.

Discussion and Shared Writing: What Things Are Made From Trees?

- Review the question of the day.

- Show some of the larger tree parts from your collection, such as tree stumps, tree cookies, or large branches.

- Explain, "Sticks, tree branches, and tree trunks are *wooden*, which means they are made from wood. We make things from wood because it is hard and strong."

- Say, "Remember that trees are living things. They grow and change. Once the tree is cut down, the wood becomes nonliving." Refer back to the list of living and nonliving things that you created during Investigation 5, "How do trees change?" Point out any nonliving, *wooden* items.

- Pass around a collection of objects, some of which are obviously made of wood, e.g., a wooden spoon or wooden toy truck, and others that are not.

- Ask children to sort the objects into two categories: things that are *wooden* and things that are not *wooden*.

- Record the names of the wooden items.

English-Language Learners

When English-language learners ask you to name a wooden object in English, ask them to tell you its name in their first languages. This strategy helps them feel like experts. It also introduces words in various languages to other children.

Before transitioning to interest areas, talk about the wood and sandpaper in the Discovery area and how children can use them.

Choice Time	As you interact with children in the interest areas, make time to do the following: • Talk to them as they experiment with the wood and sandpaper. • Take pictures of their experiments.	• Ask, "How does the wood change when you rub the sandpaper back and forth on it?" • Record their responses, and post them in the Discovery area along with photos of their experiments.
Read-Aloud	Read *A Tree Is For...* • **Before you read**, tell the title and ask, "What do you think this book is about?" • **As you read**, ask, "How do you have fun with trees?" after you read the part about "a tree is for having fun."	• **After you read**, list the things in the book that are made from trees. Tell the children that the book will be available on the computer in the Technology area.
Small Group	**Option 1: Drawing a House** • Use *Intentional Teaching Card* LL32, "Describing Art." Follow the guidance on the card. • Read *The Three Little Pigs*. • Talk about the different materials that the pigs used to construct their houses. • Discuss the two houses that were not sturdy enough to withstand the wolf's blowing. • Invite children to draw a sturdy house.	**Option 2: Building a House** • Review *Intentional Teaching Card* LL32, "Describing Art." Follow the guidance on the card. • Read *The Three Little Pigs*. • Talk about the different materials that the pigs used to construct their houses. • Discuss the two houses that were not sturdy enough to withstand the wolf's blowing. • Invite children to construct a sturdy house by using craft sticks or other small sticks and clay.
Mighty Minutes®	• Use *Mighty Minutes* 20, "I Can Make a Circle." Follow the guidance on the card.	
Large-Group Roundup	• Recall the day's events. • Invite children to show and describe the sturdy houses they created during small-group time today. • Remind the children that someone will be visiting tomorrow to explain how to build something out of wood.	• Ask, "What would you like to ask our visitor tomorrow?" • Record their questions.

Investigation 6

What can we do with parts of trees?

Vocabulary

English: See *Book Discussion Card* 16, *A Grand Old Tree*
(*El gran árbol centenario*), for words.

Question of the Day: What would you like to ask our visitor today?

Large Group

Opening Routine

- Sing a welcome song and talk about who's here.

Music: Beating Drum Patterns

- Give each child a drum, or encourage the children to find things in the room that they can use as drums.

- Remind the children how to hold their drums in a resting position until everyone is ready.

- Use *Mighty Minutes* 26, "Echo Clapping." Follow the guidance on the card, using drums.

> **Asking children to hold their instruments without playing them promotes self-regulation. You are encouraging children to inhibit a behavior (in this case, playing the drums).**

Discussion and Shared Writing: Visitor Who Makes Things From Wood

- Introduce the visitor.

- Invite the visitor to talk about how he or she uses woodworking tools and the wooden items made with them.

- Invite the children to ask their questions from yesterday's large-group roundup and any additional questions from the discussion of today's question of the day.

Before transitioning to interest areas, say, "We know that wood comes from trees." Ask, "Did you know that paper is made from trees, too?" Talk about the different kinds of paper in the Discovery area. Explain how to look closely at the paper with a magnifying glass.

Choice Time

As you interact with children in the interest areas, make time to do the following:

- Listen to children's descriptions of the paper in the Discovery area.

- Invite children to record their discoveries by drawing what they see.

> **See *Intentional Teaching Card* LL63, "Investigating & Recording," for more ideas.**

Read-Aloud

Read *A Grand Old Tree*.

- Use *Book Discussion Card* 16, *A Grand Old Tree*. Follow the guidance on the card for the first read-aloud.

Small Group

Option 1: Wooden Collections

- Use *Intentional Teaching Card* M05, "Sorting & Classifying."

- Invite each child to collect a few objects in the classroom.

- Follow the guidance on the card. Invite the children to sort the objects into two categories: things that are wooden and things that are not.

Option 2: Wood Hunt

- Use *Intentional Teaching Card* M05, "Sorting & Classifying."

- Invite children to hunt for wood with you around the school.

- Have the children identify wooden objects and take pictures of them.

- Return to the classroom to view and print the photos together.

- Follow the guidance on the card to help the children sort into categories the photos of the found objects.

- Use the photos to create a book of wooden objects around the school.

Mighty Minutes®

- Use *Mighty Minutes* 18, "I'm Thinking Of..." Follow the guidance on the card.

Large-Group Roundup

- Recall the day's events.

- Write a group thank-you note to the woodworker who visited today.

What can we do with parts of trees?

Vocabulary

English: *wooden*

Spanish: *de madera*

Question of the Day: Is our school made from wood?

Large Group

Opening Routine

- Sing a welcome song and talk about who's here.

Game: 1, 2, 3, What Do I See?

- Use *Mighty Minutes* 50, "1, 2, 3, What Do I See?" Follow the guidance on the card.

Discussion and Shared Writing: Woodworking Tools

- Remind children about yesterday's visitor who makes things out of wood.

- Ask the children to recall what tools the visitor uses to work with wood.

- Record their responses.

- Review the question of the day.

Before transitioning to interest areas, talk about the wood and woodworking tools available in the Discovery area and how children can use them.

> Before letting children use woodworking tools, make sure they know how to handle them safely. You may want to have a family volunteer or another adult help you supervise the children.

Choice Time

As you interact with children in the interest areas, make time to do the following:

- Observe children as they work with the wood. Ask questions about their constructions and how they made them.

- Offer assistance and safety reminders as needed.

> Conflicts arise in every classroom. When children come to you because of a conflict, you can help them learn to express their feelings appropriately and learn skills to resolve the problem on their own. For more information, see *Intentional Teaching Card* SE13, "Conflict Resolution."

Read-Aloud

Read *A Tree Is For....*

- **Before you read**, talk about the pictures on the front cover of the book and what they tell about the story.

- **As you read**, talk about the details of the pictures.

- **After you read**, ask, "What is a tree for?" Record their responses.

Small Group

Option 1: A Closer Look at Wood

- Use *Intentional Teaching Card* LL63, "Investigating & Recording."

- Follow the guidance on the card. Invite children to explore the collection of wooden objects in the classroom.

Option 2: Close Up Outdoors

- Review *Intentional Teaching Card* LL63, "Investigating & Recording."

- Follow the guidance on the card.

- Take the children outdoors. Invite them to locate wooden objects and explore them closely.

Mighty Minutes®

- Use *Mighty Minutes* 57, "Find the Letter Sound." Try the shape variation on the back of the card.

Large-Group Roundup

- Recall the day's events.

- Invite children to share what they discovered during their investigation of wooden objects during small-group time today.

Investigation 6

What can we do with parts of trees?

Vocabulary

English: See *Book Discussion Card* 16, *A Grand Old Tree* (*El gran árbol centenario*), for additional words.

Question of the Day: Which wooden instrument would you like to play? (Display two or three different instruments.)

Large Group

Opening Routine

- Sing a welcome song and talk about who's here.

Music: Beating Drum Patterns

- Give each child a drum, or encourage the children to find things in the room that they can use as drums.

- Remind the children how to hold their drums in a resting position until everyone is ready.

- Use *Mighty Minutes* 26, "Echo Clapping."

- Follow the guidance on the card, using drums.

Discussion and Shared Writing: Exploring Wooden Instruments

- Provide a collection of wooden instruments for the children to explore.

- Talk about the different kinds of instruments that are made from wood. If possible, show the children some pictures of wooden instruments that you do not have in the classroom.

- Invite children to look closely at how the instruments are made. Invite them to play the instruments that they find interesting.

- Review the question of the day.

- Give the children plenty of time to explore the different instruments.

- Ask, "What can you tell me about these instruments?

- Record their responses.

> Introduce the instruments in the way that will work best for your group. For example, you may choose to pass around one or two of the same kind of instrument. Alternatively, you might pass around a basket of different instruments and allow each child to select one.

Before transitioning to interest areas, explain that the instruments will be available in the Music and Movement area. Discuss how the children can use them.

Choice Time

As you interact with children in the interest areas, make time to do the following:

- Watch and listen as children explore the instruments.

- If possible, record the children playing the instruments.

> For more information on engaging children during choice time, see *The Creative Curriculum® for Preschool, Volume 1: The Foundation.*

Read-Aloud

Read *A Grand Old Tree*.

- Use *Book Discussion Card* 16, *A Grand Old Tree.* Follow the guidance on the card for the second read-aloud.

Small Group

Option 1: Tallying

- Use *Intentional Teaching Card* M06, "Tallying."

- Follow the guidance on the card.

- Invite children to tally the wooden items they find in a selected interest area.

Option 2: Graphing

- Use *Intentional Teaching Card* M11, "Graphing."

- Follow the guidance on the card. Invite children to help you graph the number of wooden items they find in each of several interest areas.

Mighty Minutes®

- Use *Mighty Minutes* 55, "Mr. Forgetful." Follow the guidance on the card.

Large-Group Roundup

- Recall the day's events.

- Invite children who explored wooden instruments in the Music and Movement area today to play them. If you were able to record the children as they played the instruments, play the recording, and discuss the different sounds.

Additional Questions to Investigate

If children are still engaged in this study and want to find out more, you might investigate additional questions. Here are some suggestions:

- "Which trees grow the tallest?"

- "Where is the biggest tree in the world?"

- "Why do the leaves change color?"

- "What do trees do when it does not rain for a long time?"

- "How long do different types of trees live?"

- "Trees stay in one place, so how do their seeds get to different places?"

- "Do trees do anything special to attract creatures that are helpful to them?"

Are there additional questions that will help you extend this study?

Our Investigation

Our Investigation

	Day 1	Day 2	Day 3
Interest Areas			
Question of the Day			
Large Group			
Read-Aloud			
Small Group			
Mighty Minutes®			

Day 4	Day 5	Make Time for...
		Outdoor Experiences
		Family Partnerships
		Wow! Experiences

Our Investigation

Vocabulary
English:
Spanish:

Large Group

Vocabulary

Choice Time

Read-Aloud

Small Group

Mighty Minutes®

Large-Group
Roundup

Celebrating Learning

Closing the Study

When the study ends—when most of the children's questions have been answered—it is important to reflect and celebrate. Plan a special way to celebrate their learning and accomplishments. Allow children to assume as much responsibility as possible for planning the activities. Here are some suggestions:

- Set up stations in interest areas for children to show visitors how they investigated trees.

- Have the children set up a self-serve snack bar featuring foods grown on trees, e.g., apples, peaches, pears, oranges, grapefruits, dates, figs, and assorted tree nuts. Be mindful of children's food allergies. Invite family members to participate.

- Create a display, called "See How We've Grown!" Compare children's height as babies and as they are now using the masking tape they marked.

- Invite families to an informal picnic under the trees in the play yard. Feature tree-grown foods.

- Make a class book, photo album, documentation panel, or slide show about the trees study.

- Invite families to join the children in an outdoor game of hide-and-seek among the trees.

- Create a display of various tree homes and have children draw pictures of their inhabitants. Place the drawings beside their respective tree homes.

- Record a video of children interviewing each other about what they've learned. Show the video to the children's families.

- Invite families to an informal recital featuring the children playing various wooden instruments.

- The following pages provide daily plans for two days of celebration. Add your ideas and the children's ideas for how best to celebrate their learning.

Celebrating Learning

Vocabulary—English: *celebration*

	Day 1	Day 2	
Interest Areas	**All:** displays of children's investigations	**Discovery:** small trees or tree seeds; pots; potting soil **All:** displays of children's investigations	
Question of the Day	What would you like to show our guests about the trees study at the celebration tomorrow?	What was your favorite part of the study?	
Large Group	**Rhyme:** "Come Play With Me" **Discussion and Shared Writing:** Preparing for the Celebration **Materials:** *Mighty Minutes* 42, "Come Play With Me"	**Song:** "The Green Grass Grows" **Discussion and Shared Writing:** Memories About Trees **Materials:** *Mighty Minutes* 54, "The Green Grass Grows" **Large-Group Roundup Materials:** *Intentional Teaching Card* SE26, "Making a Mural" (for large-group roundup)	
Read-Aloud	*Pablo's Tree*	*A Grand Old Tree* *Book Discussion Card* 16 (third read-aloud)	
Small Group	**Option 1: Applesauce** *Intentional Teaching Card* M28, "Applesauce" (See card for equipment, recipe, and ingredients.) **Option 2: Apple Bread** *Intentional Teaching Card* M29, "Apple Bread" (See card for equipment, recipe, and ingredients.)	**Option 1: A Shared Story About Trees** *Intentional Teaching Card* LL01, "Shared Writing" **Option 2: Our Tree Book** *Intentional Teaching Card* LL02, "Desktop Publishing"; digital camera; computer; printer; each child's individual word bank; bookbinding supplies	
Mighty Minutes®	*Mighty Minutes* 96, "This Old Man"	*Mighty Minutes* 49, "A Tree My Size"	

Make Time for...

Outdoor Experiences

Plant a Tree

• At the celebration, invite families to join you as you plant one or more trees outside in the play yard.

Physical Fun

• Use *Intentional Teaching Card* P14, "Moving Through the Forest." Follow the guidance on the card.

Family Partnerships

• Invite families to attend the celebration.

Wow! Experiences

• Day 2: Family members visit for the celebration.

Day 1   Celebrating Learning

Let's plan our celebration

Vocabulary

English: *celebration*

Spanish: *celebración*

Question of the Day: What would you like to show our guests about the trees study at the celebration tomorrow?

Large Group

Opening Routine

- Sing a welcome song and talk about who's here.

Rhyme: "Come Play With Me"

- Use *Mighty Minutes* 42, "Come Play With Me." Follow the guidance on the card.

Discussion and Shared Writing: Preparing for the Celebration

- Talk about tomorrow's celebration.

- Review the question of the day.

- Ask the children what they would like to show their families and friends about what they learned during the study.

- Record their responses.

Before transitioning to interest areas, tell children that you will help them gather the items from the list to create displays for family and friends to see tomorrow at the celebration.

Choice Time

As you interact with children in the interest areas, make time to do the following:

- Help children gather the items they would like to share at the celebration.

Read-Aloud

Read *Pablo's Tree.*

- **Before you read**, ask, "Who remembers what this story is about?"

- **As you read**, comment on how happy Lito was when he heard that Pablo's mother was going to adopt a baby and how excited he was to finally meet his grandson, Pablo.

- **After you read**, ask, "What kind of presents do people usually give to a new baby? Why do they give those things? Why do you think Lito bought a small tree for Pablo?"

> **Asking open-ended questions encourages children to use their imaginations.**

Small Group

Option 1: Applesauce

- Use *Intentional Teaching Card* M28, "Applesauce." Follow the guidance on the card.

Option 2: Apple Bread

- Use *Intentional Teaching Card* M29, "Apple Bread." Follow the guidance on the card.

> **Save the food that you made together during small-group time to share with families at tomorrow's celebration. The children will enjoy sharing something they prepared themselves.**

Mighty Minutes®

- Use *Mighty Minutes* 96, "This Old Man." Try the silly rhyming variation on the back.

Large-Group Roundup

- Recall the day's events.

- Remind the children that there will be a special celebration tomorrow.

Let's celebrate

Vocabulary

English: See *Book Discussion Card* 16, *A Grand Old Tree* (*El gran árbol centenario*), for words.

Question of the Day: What was your favorite part of the study?

Large Group

Opening Routine

• Sing a welcome song and talk about who's here.

Song: "The Green Grass Grows"

• Use *Mighty Minutes* 54, "The Green Grass Grows." Follow the guidance on the card.

Discussion and Shared Writing: Memories About Trees

• Welcome families to the celebration.

• Invite families to share any special stories about trees.

• Refer to the question of the day. Invite the children to share their favorite parts of the study with their guests.

• Record what they say about the study.

Before transitioning to interest areas, talk about the small trees or tree seeds and pots in the Discovery area. Discuss how and where the children can plant them.

Choice Time

As you interact with children in the interest areas, make time to do the following:

• Invite children to talk to the family members and other visitors about their work that is displayed around the room.

English-Language Learners
Some English-language learners may prefer to talk with family members and visitors in their first languages. This can support their confidence in social situations. It also helps introduce different languages to English-speaking children.

Read-Aloud

Read *A Grand Old Tree*.

- Use *Book Discussion Card* 16, *A Grand Old Tree.* Follow the guidance on the card for the third read-aloud.

Small Group

Option 1: A Shared Story About Trees

- Use *Intentional Teaching Card* LL01, "Shared Writing."

- Follow the guidance on the card.

- Invite children to make up a story about the art display that they created throughout the study.

Option 2: Our Tree Book

- Use *Intentional Teaching Card* LL02, "Desktop Publishing."

- Take digital photos of different parts of the art display.

- Follow the guidance on the card. Have the children use the photos to write and illustrate a story about the display.

Mighty Minutes®

- Use *Mighty Minutes* 49, "A Tree My Size." Follow the guidance on the card.

Large-Group Roundup

- Recall the day's events.

- See *Intentional Teaching Card* SE26, "Making a Mural." Invite the children to create a thank-you mural for the guests. Post the mural in the classroom.

Reflecting on the Study

What were the most engaging parts of the study?

Are there other topics that might be worth investigating?

If I were to change any part of the study, it would be:

Other thoughts and ideas I have:

Resources

Background Information for Teachers

What is a tree? A tree is a *perennial* plant. Perennial plants typically live longer than two years. Trees usually have a single main trunk that supports multiple branches. Their structure is different from bushes, which are also perennials but usually have several stems at the base.

Some trees are *deciduous* and lose their leaves in certain seasons. Other trees are *evergreen*, which means that their leaves and needles stay green, and the tree keeps most of them all year. Each type, or *species*, of tree has specific needs and must have the right *habitat* to thrive. A habitat is a type of environment, such as a desert or forest, in which a plant or animal lives.

Consider why trees are important.

- **Trees help us breathe.** They improve the quality of our air by converting carbon dioxide into oxygen. They also act as natural air filters that remove certain pollutants from the air.

- **Trees provide food**, such as fruits and nuts. They also grow berries and flowers, which feed many insects and other animals.

- **Trees provide shelter.** They are home to a wide variety of animals and sometimes people.

- **Trees reduce soil erosion.** The roots of a tree help keep the soil in place after a hard rain.

- **Trees provide materials.** People use the materials from trees to make many things, such as paper, furniture, medications, tools, homes, and other buildings.

- **Trees reduce our energy needs.** In warmer months, they provide shade to keep our homes cool. In the winter, many lose their leaves and allow the sun's heat to shine through.

Trees have many parts that serve a specific purpose.

- *Roots* hold the trunk firmly in the ground and grow outward like branches underneath the soil. The roots absorb water and minerals from the soil and transport them to the trunk of the tree.

- The *trunk* is the main stem of the tree. It carries water and minerals to the rest of the branches.

- *Bark* is a tree's tough outer layer that protects it from harmful insects and diseases. Bark varies in thicknesses, color, and texture.

- The *branches* hold up the leaves to ensure the best possible exposure to sunlight. The branches also carry water and minerals to the leaves. Many places on the branches end in *twigs*, out of which the leaves grow.

- *Leaves* make food for the tree from a gas found in the air, water, and sunlight. They make their food through *photosynthesis,* a chemical process.

- Some trees have *flowers*, which play an important role in reproduction.

Trees are divided into two main groups.

- *Conifers* are trees that have needle- or scale-like leaves and cones. Conifer seeds are found in the cones. Some conifers, such as junipers, have soft, fleshy cone scales that look like berries.

- *Broadleaf* trees, such as maples, do not have cones. Instead, their seeds are typically contained inside a fruit, berry, nut, or pod.

What do you want to research to help you understand this topic?

Children's Books

In addition to the children's books specifically used in this *Teaching Guide*, you may wish to supplement daily activities and interest areas with some of the listed children's books.

A Friend for All Seasons (Julie Hubery)

A Tree for Me (Nancy Van Laan)

A Tree Is Nice (Janice May Udry)

Aani and the Tree Huggers (Jeannine Atkins)

Animal Poems of the Iguazú/Animalario del Iguazú (Francisco X. Alarcón)

Another Tree in the Yard (Lucia Sera)

At Grandpa's Sugar Bush (Margaret Carney)

At the Edge of the Woods: A Counting Book (Cynthia Cotton)

El Bosque (Claire Nivola)

Cherry Tree (Ruskin Bond)

Curious George Plants a Tree (H.A. Rey)

Everybody Needs a Hideaway (Dean Bennett)

Fernando's Gift: El regalo de Fernando (Douglas Keister)

The First Forest (John Gile)

El flamboyan amarillo (Georgina Lazaro)

The Forest (Claire Nivola)

The Gift of the Tree (Alvin Tresselt)

The Giving Tree (Shel Silverstein)

The Grandad Tree (Trish Cooke)

The Great Kapok Tree: A Tale of the Amazon Rain Forest (Lynn Cherry)

Gus Is a Tree (Claire Babin)

Hello Willow (Kimberly Poulton)

Isabel's House of Butterflies (Tony Johnston)

Leaf Man (Lois Ehlert)

The Legend of the African Bao-Bab Tree (Bobbi Dooley Hunter)

The Lorax (Dr. Seuss)

Lost in the Woods: A Photographic Fantasy (Carl Sams)

Leaves (David Ezra Stein)

Little Bent Cedar (Bryan Speed)

The Man Who Lived in a Hollow Tree (Anne Shelby)

My Great Grandmother's Gourd (Cristina Kessler)

Napí (Antonio Ramirez)

Night Tree (Eve Bunting)

El niño y el arbol (Vivi Escriva)

Niwechihaw/I Help (Caitlin Dale Nicholson)

One Small Square: Woods (Donald Silver)

Pascual's Magic Pictures (Amy Glaser Gage)

Pearl Plants a Tree (Jane Breskin Zalben)

Prairie Willow (Maxine Trottier)

The Seasons of Arnold's Apple Tree (Gail Gibbons)

Tell Me, Tree: All About Trees for Kids (Gail Gibbons)

The Tree (Karen Gray Ruelle)

Tree Crazy (Tracy Gallup)

The Tree Farmer (Chuck Leavell and Nicholas Cravotta)

The Tree in the Wood: An Old Nursery Song (Christopher Manson)

Trees to Paper (Welcome Books) (Inez Snyder)

The Umbrella Queen (Shirin Yim Bridges)

Up in the Tree (Margaret Atwood)

Up, Up, Down! (Robert Munsch)

Verdi (Janell Cannon)

The Way of the Willow Branch (Emery Bernhard)

We're Going on a Leaf Hunt (Steve Metzger)

While a Tree Was Growing (Jane Bosveld)

Teacher Resources

The teacher resources provide additional information and ideas for enhancing and extending the study topic.

Arbor Day: The Holiday That Makes a Difference, video (The Arbor Day Foundation)

The Tree Book for Kids and Their Grown Ups (Gina Ingoglia)

Trees (Pocket Guides, DK Publishers)

Trees, Leaves and Bark (Take-Along Guide, Diane L. Burns)

Weekly Planning Form

Week of: _____ Teacher: _____ Study: _____

	Monday	Tuesday	Wednesday	Thursday	Friday
Interest Areas					
Large Group					
Read-Aloud					
Small Group					

Outdoor Experiences:

Family Partnerships:

Wow! Experiences:

Weekly Planning Form, continued

"To Do" List:

Reflecting on the week:

Individual Child Planning